CITYSPOTS
KUALA

WHAT'S IN YOUR GUIDEBOOK?

Independent authors Impartial up-to-date information from our travel experts who meticulously source local knowledge.

Experience Thomas Cook's 165 years in the travel industry and guidebook publishing enriches every word with expertise you can trust.

Travel know-how Thomas Cook has thousands of staff working around the globe, all living and breathing travel.

Editors Travel-publishing professionals, pulling everything together to craft a perfect blend of words, pictures, maps and design.

You, the traveller We deliver a practical, no-nonsense approach to information, geared to how you really use it.

CITYSPOTS
KUALA LUMPUR

Thomas Cook

Written by Pat Levy
Updated by Michelle Balmer

Published by Thomas Cook Publishing
A division of Thomas Cook Tour Operations Limited
Company registration No: 3772199 England
The Thomas Cook Business Park, 9 Coningsby Road
Peterborough PE3 8SB, United Kingdom
Email: books@thomascook.com, Tel: +44 (0)1733 416477
www.thomascookpublishing.com

Produced by The Content Works Ltd
Aston Court, Kingsmead Business Park, Frederick Place
High Wycombe, Bucks HP11 1LA
www.thecontentworks.com

Series design based on an original concept by Studio 183 Limited

ISBN: 978-1-84848-174-9

First edition © 2007 Thomas Cook Publishing
This second edition © 2009 Thomas Cook Publishing
Text © Thomas Cook Publishing
Maps © Thomas Cook Publishing/PCGraphics (UK) Limited
Transport map © Communicarta Limited

Series Editor: Lucy Armstrong
Production/DTP: Steven Collins

Printed and bound in Spain by GraphyCems

Cover photography (Sultan Abdul Samad Building) © PCL/Alamy

CONTENTS

SYMBOLS KEY

The following symbols are used throughout this book:

ⓐ address ☏ telephone ⓦ website address ⓛ opening times
ⓝ public transport connections ❶ important

The following symbols are used on the maps:

ℹ️ information office		▪ points of interest	
✈ airport		○ city	
➕ hospital		○ large town	
🛡 police station		○ small town	
🚍 bus station		= motorway	
🚆 railway station		— main road	
Ⓜ Monorail Stop		— minor road	
Ⓜ Ampang Line Stop		— railway	
Ⓜ Kelana Jaya Line Stop		❶ numbers denote featured	
✝ cathedral		cafés & restaurants	

Hotels and restaurants are graded by approximate price as follows:
£ budget price ££ mid-range price £££ expensive

▶ *The view from the Petronas Towers Skybridge*

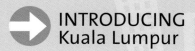

Introduction

The first impression one gets of Kuala Lumpur, on arrival at the ultra-modern international airport, KLIA, is that it is typical of the new, 21st-century face of Asia. But although it might look disconcertingly like the modern face of the continent you have just left – and catching the sleek KLIA Ekspres train into Sentral Station may offer few surprises – the taxi ride to your hotel will soon alert you to what is different, as the driver negotiates horrendous traffic with disarming aplomb, ducking down impossibly narrow side streets before emerging suddenly outside a smart-looking hotel.

As you take a first stroll through the streets, the humidity hits you like a brick wall – that refreshing shower you took will count for nothing – and the sudden strangeness of the city begins to assert itself. There are alluring shopping malls and shining skyscrapers, for sure, and you are unlikely to forget first seeing the metallic splendour of the Petronas Towers, but ordinary street life will prove at least equally engaging.

Kuala Lumpur is a city with attitude, but seems unaware of it: what you see is what you get. This might mean a ride in a clapped-out taxi with the air conditioning not working or an indifferent attitude when trying to get information but it could also mean an honest smile, a keen willingness to assist and an easy-going manner that helps you relax easily and really enjoy your visit. Remember too that once you arrive in Kuala Lumpur you immediately earn the right to refer to the city simply as KL. This is what everyone else calls their city, and part of the fun of being there is learning more about the Malaysian and KL way of life, perhaps picking up some of the local ways yourself.

⬤ *The Petronas Towers are the modern face of KL*

When to go

SEASONS & CLIMATE

There is no season of the year when the traveller to Kuala
Lumpur is disadvantaged. There is a so-called rainy season
between October and April, but you will not notice this in the
capital. The occasionally heavy shower of rain, which invariably
ceases after an hour or two, is less common between May and
September but can still occur any time of the year. The real
constant is the tropical climate, and this means that the
temperature rarely goes below 20°C (68°F), even through the
night, and readings above 30°C (86°F) are the norm during the
middle part of the day. It is not just the heat but the high
humidity, always around 90 per cent, that takes some getting
used to, and it is important to adjust your pace when walking –
don't walk too briskly and think about the time of day when
setting out somewhere on foot. Even a short walk around
midday and in the full sun can be debilitating. Sunglasses or
a peaked cap provide welcome shade and you should always
carry a supply of water.

ANNUAL EVENTS

Malaysia celebrates festivals relating to the country's different
cultures and religions and this means a fairly packed calendar.
Some have fixed dates but many are based around the lunar
calendar, so the actual dates vary from one year to the next.

January–February

See page 14 for the **Chinese New Year** and **Thaipusam**. The

🔺 *Thousands of devotees and onlookers gather to celebrate Thaipusam*

highlights of 1 February, **Federal Territory Day**, are cultural performances and a grand fireworks display.

March–May

Easter passes fairly unnoticed, the city's Christian community being quite a small one, but **Vesak Day** in May is more conspicuous. Take a taxi to the Maha Vahara Buddhist temple in Brickfields, 2 km (1¼ miles) south of the Central Market, to see the celebrations. Caged birds are released and the scent of joss sticks fills the air to mark the Buddha's birth, enlightenment and death.

June–August

The Chinese **Festival of the Hungry Ghosts** in late August is an interesting time to visit Chinatown. Paper money is burnt as offerings and improvised shrines appear by the roadside, filled with token gifts of food and burning joss sticks. **National Day** at the end of August is the day to be in Merdeka Square for colourful displays and processions representing the country's different states. In Chinatown, the **Mooncake Festival** is celebrated by eating the eponymous cakes which are on sale everywhere. Only buy one to sample, though: as the euphemism goes, enjoying them is an acquired taste. Another Chinese festival, the **Nine Emperor Gods Festival**, is a colourful affair held at temples, when a procession marks the return of the nine gods to their heavenly abode. The major Muslim festival of **Ramadan** brings a month-long fasting period from dawn to dusk. Non-Muslims are not required to participate and most of the city's restaurants continue to operate as normal. While Muslim restaurants mostly remain open, the best time to visit one is during the evening, when families flock to them to break their fast.

September–December
In autumn, **Deepavali** is a heartening time to visit Hindu temples, celebrating as they do the triumph of good deeds over evil ones.

Christmas is more a commercial celebration than a religious one, but big hotels will mount their own celebrations and it is worth looking out for restaurant promotions.

PUBLIC HOLIDAYS
All Muslim festivals are lunar-related, so dates vary.
New Year's Day 1 Jan
Chinese New Year 14 & 15 Feb 2010, 3 & 4 Feb 2011
Thaipusam 8 Feb
Labour Day 1 May
Vesak Day 28 Apr 2010, 10 May 2011
King's birthday First Sat in June
National Day 31 Aug
Hari Raya Puasa 20 Sept 2009, 10 Sept 2010, 30 Aug 2011
Deepavali 17 Oct 2009, 5 Nov 2010, 26 Oct 2011
Hari Raya Haji 27 Nov 2009, 16 Nov 2010, 10 Nov 2011
Muslim New Year 27 Dec 2009, 18 Dec 2010, 16 Dec 2011
Christmas Day 25 Dec

Special events

CHINESE NEW YEAR

Two days are officially put aside for the Chinese New Year. During this time, all Chinese-run businesses close down. The days leading up to Chinese New Year are the busiest time of the year in Chinatown; everyone buys decorations and special foods. Look out for a noisy and colourful lion dance and, less common, a Chinese opera performance on a makeshift stage in Chinatown. For maximum impact, visit Petaling Street on the eve of Chinese New Year and the feverish atmosphere will make itself felt, though the crowds can be a little overwhelming. The week leading up to the two days of public holiday is a time when Chinese restaurants are always full and reservations will be essential. It is also a time when public transport out of the capital is fully booked: bear this in mind if planning a trip to Melaka.

THAIPUSAM

Thaipusam, commemorating the day when the goddess Parvathi gave her son Murugan a weapon for defeating the evil demons, takes the form of a procession from the Sri Mahamariamman Temple (see page 82) to Batu Caves (see page 116). Devotees pierce their bodies with *kavadis*, metal frames attached by steel hooks to the bare skin. Some participants will have skewers through their cheeks or tongues; the event has to be seen to be believed. By the time the procession reaches Batu Caves, approximately one million people will be watching, so most visitors will find it less taxing to watch the start of the procession from the Hindu temple in the city.

DEEPAVALI

Deepavali, or Divali, is a very popular Hindu celebration also known as the Festival of Lights. It usually falls in October or November. Earthern lamps are burned; the light signifies goodness, driving out darkness and evil. While most Hindus celebrate Deepavali in their homes with family and friends, visitors should be on the lookout for lighting displays, and *kolams* – colourful paintings of rice powder – that can be found on footpaths around the city.

◆ *Deepavali celebrations are colourful and lively*

History

Kuala Lumpur's history dates back to 1857, when a group of Chinese tin miners, seeking new deposits of the valuable metal, set up camp at the confluence of the Klang and Gombak rivers. It was an unknown spot of no previous importance to Malay rulers, or to the British, who were present in nearby Melaka (Malacca). The deposits of tin were plentiful; miners flocked to the area and a settlement developed.

By the 1880s, Kuala Lumpur was a prosperous small town. The British were lured in by the profits to be made. Rubber plantations were established in the area, bringing immigrants from India, and railway lines were laid down. By 1914 the whole of peninsular Malaysia, then called Malaya, was under British rule, and Kuala Lumpur developed into the capital of the colony.

Change came with World War II and the landing of Japanese forces in the northeast of the country. British-led forces were ill-prepared to deal with the invasion and the capital was abandoned in the rush to retreat down the peninsula to Singapore. When the war ended in 1945, the British returned and resumed their colonial rule, but three years later a war of independence broke out, conducted largely by the country's Chinese, who sought a communist state. The British managed to contain the insurgents, partly militarily and partly by conceding power to non-communist Malay nationalists.

Independence came to Malaysia in 1957, but discontent between the Chinese and the Malays, brought about by the unwillingness of Malays to accept the Chinese as politically equal, reached breaking point in 1969. The outbreak of serious riots in Kuala Lumpur left many people dead. A Malay-led government introduced positive discrimination in order to redress the economic imbalance that was at the heart of anti-Chinese resentment.

The 1990s witnessed a tremendous economic boom in Malaysia. The completion of the Petronas Towers in 1989, then the world's tallest building, was visual confirmation of the country's aspirations. It came at a cost: for political opposition was dealt with severely by prime minister Mahathir Mohamad. Mahathir stepped down in 2003, but government policies have remained broadly the same. Kuala Lumpur continues to thrive as the centre of a pro-Western economy.

⬤ *Celebrating independence on National Day*

Lifestyle

You could be forgiven for thinking that eating and shopping constitute the core of KL's lifestyle. Whether it be young professionals hanging out in Bangsar and Jalan Doraisamy, taxi drivers breaking off work for noodles or to enjoy *roti* by a pavement table, or shoppers streaming in to the food centres, the enjoyment

● *Garland-making: part of the multicultural lifestyle in KL*

of eating outside the home is a constant feature of the capital's lifestyle. The multicultural background, plus the influence of Western cuisines, provides a rich variety of food tastes; the different ethnic groups, far from being tied down to their own culture's cuisine, are brought together in the common enjoyment of each other's favourite dishes.

Shopping is another activity that cuts across social and ethnic divides, especially with the young. However, visitors are advised to stay clear of the shopping malls at weekends unless they enjoy feeling like sardines in a can. The popularity of eating and shopping is increased by the opportunities they provide for families to be together. Kuala Lumpur is a hard-working city where for most people the hours of employment are long. Leisure time therefore provides a chance for friends and families to get together and enjoy some quality time.

Kuala Lumpur, like the country as a whole, is home to three distinct ethnic groups. Malays are numerically the largest, making up about 44 per cent of the city's population. In the city centre, however, the Chinese and Indian communities seem as numerous. This is partly because the Chinese have a disproportionate presence in the commercial field and partly, too, because the attraction of Indian food and temples increases the presence of what is the smallest of the three ethnic groups. The multiculturalism of the capital is an endearing feature of the city's lifestyle – mutual tolerance runs deep and there is remarkably little sense of any ethnic divisions. Malays, Chinese and Indians work and eat together, and live side by side in the same neighbourhoods, and it is only at times of religious festivals that the different cultural identities assert themselves.

Culture

Malays were – and still are to a large extent – the traditional farmers and fishermen of the country, living in small *kampungs* (villages) made up of wooden houses built above the ground on platforms held up by large stilts. You can still catch glimpses of this culture if taking an excursion outside of the city. The villagers' traditional dress – the wrap-around cotton garment called the sarong – has made a successful transition to urban life in the form of fashionable and very colourful versions that are worn both informally and formally. Being Muslims, Malays celebrate the main religious holidays – although in fact you could be in KL during the fasting month of Ramadan and hardly notice it – and mosques are always busy on Fridays. The wearing of a veil is rare in Kuala Lumpur, although some form of headdress is common among female Malays.

The Chinese have retained a strong presence in the city they founded. They first came to the Malay Peninsula in the 13th century, escaping dire poverty, and a strong work ethic born out of the need to survive remains a characteristic of the culture. So too does a respect for tradition, and events like the Chinese New Year reveal the depth of attachment to their cultural roots. At any time of the year, wonderfully unreconstructed Chinatown is worth exploring for the many windows it opens on Chinese culture. The See Yeoh Temple, one of the most interesting in the city, is also to be found here.

Indians first came to KL in the late 19th century as labourers, mostly from south India, and while many Tamils still work in the construction industry, it is their impact on the capital's food

⬤ *Chinese temples reflect the cultural roots of the city*

scene that you are most likely to experience directly. Religious festivals like Thaipusam and Deepavali contribute much to the city's dramatic and colourful cultural calendar.

A feature common to the Malay, Chinese and Indian populations in the city is their adherence to traditional forms of worship, most obvious when visiting a mosque or a temple. This does not breed intolerance, however, and cultural interchange between the different groups operates at a sophisticated level, although mixed marriages are still not common.

There is a sizeable number of Western expatriates in the city, though Western culture makes its strongest impact in the form of the Hollywood blockbusters shown at the many cinemas, and the drinking culture centred in entertainment areas around Bukit Bintang and Jalan Doraisamy. There is also the fascinating mixed-group Peranakan culture, formed historically by marriages between Chinese settlers and local Malay women, which makes itself felt in the unique food dishes that evolved in the process.

▶ *The Sultan Abdul Samad Building*

MAKING THE MOST OF
Kuala Lumpur

Shopping

Shopping is a very good reason for visiting Kuala Lumpur: prices for merchandise of reasonable-to-good quality are some of the best to be found anywhere in Asia. When prices are clearly displayed, usually the case in the big shopping malls, there is no need to engage in protracted bargaining sessions in order to obtain a reasonable deal. When prices not displayed, the first price quoted is likely to be close to what the vendor expects to receive, but some gentle, polite negotiation will often see a reduction of somewhere between 10 and 20 per cent. This will be the case for most of the shops in Central Market and for arts and crafts shops around the city. When it comes to the street market in Petaling Street, however, you need to hone your bargaining skills more sharply, because the asking price may be outrageously over the top.

⬤ *Bukit Bintang is a great place to shop*

Some of the best deals relate to cosmetics, eyewear, electronics, fabrics, fashion clothes and perfume. Batik fabrics, hand-drawn or with printed patterns, handmade silver items from regions of peninsular Malaysia and pewter ware from the Royal Selangor company are all worth considering. Arts and crafts from the states of Sarawak and Sabah in East Malaysia are another big draw. Look out especially for craft products – gift boxes, handbags, table and floor mats – woven from pandanus leaves.

There are two main shopping areas in KL: Bukit Bintang and KLCC (Kuala Lumpur City Centre). Bukit Bintang, also designated the Golden Triangle area, is home to major shopping plazas such as Sungei Wang, hugely popular with Malaysians and overseas visitors, and BB Plaza, as well as more upmarket malls like Lot 10 and Starhill Gallery. One stop away on the KL monorail line brings you to Imbi and the vast Berjaya Times Square. The KLCC shopping scene is concentrated in Suria KLCC, next to the Petronas Towers.

A minimum 15-minute cab ride from the city centre, near Bangsar, will have you arriving at Mid Valley City, a dizzyingly mammoth retail space made up of two interconnected shopping malls, **Mid Valley Megamall** and **The Gardens** (ⓐ Lingkaran Syed Putra ☎ (03) 2938 3333 ⓦ www.midvalley.com.my). Many of the shops they contain can be found within the city but if you're looking for an all-in-one retail experience and don't mind a journey, this might appeal. Avoid weekends when it becomes exceptionally crowded.

For street shopping, Petaling Street market is the main attraction, and especially so at night, when the place is heaving with shoppers looking for a bargain. If you are looking for gifts and souvenirs, you would be better off shopping in Central Market.

Eating & drinking

When it comes to eating and drinking, KL really comes into its own, presenting a diverse range of authentic cuisines from southeast Asia, plus quality Western-style dining, all at astonishingly affordable rates.

Chinese food is everywhere, and the tastiest dishes are often stir-fry ones served up quickly from a wok. You will see this for yourself in any of the food courts; the same process also takes place out of sight in the kitchens of more expensive Chinese restaurants. Lunch often takes the form of small snacks, called dim sum, served from a trolley; take pot luck if unsure which ones to choose, or ask for *pau*, steamed rice dumplings.

Malay cooking is best enjoyed from outlets in one of the many food courts, and there are a number of home favourites that should be sampled, including the classic *nasi lemak*. To say it is rice cooked in coconut milk makes it seem bland – there are subtle flavours at work here, including lemon grass, garlic, tamarind and chilli.

For the least expensive food, head for one of the many

PRICE CATEGORIES

In this book the approximate price bands into which meals at restaurants fall are based on the average cost of a three-course meal for one person, excluding drinks, and are indicated by these symbols:

£ up to RM25   ££ RM25–75   £££ over RM75

● *Cuisine meets art*

● *Street food is available day and night*

VEGETARIAN FOOD

Vegetarians should never be at a loss in Kuala Lumpur and, on the contrary, will be delighted by the range of possibilities. Every food court will have at least one dedicated vegetarian outlet, usually Chinese, where stir-fry dishes using tofu are served up in an instant. Indian restaurants are always a good bet – biryani dishes are usually available without meat – and the streetside cafés that offer *murtabak* will conjure up one without meat if you ask for it. Malay food includes *tahu goring*, made from bean sprouts and tofu with a peanut sauce, and *rojak* is a vegetarian salad that makes for a light lunch. Most restaurants can come up with vegetarian surprises that will not always appear on the menu, so always ask. For superb vegetarian Thai food, My Thai (see page 100), is sheer heaven.

Malay and Indian restaurants serving Muslim dishes in non-air-conditioned cafés. These are readily spotted because of their open access from the street pavement and the large hotplate on view at the front. It is here that you should try a firm Malaysian favourite, *roti canai*, for breakfast or a mid-morning break. *Roti canai* is a wheatflour pancake. Look for a man kneading, flattening and then slapping onto a large hot plate a mixture of flour, sugar and milk. When it includes an egg, it is called *roti telur*, but either way it is a tasty repast when dipped in the accompanying, mildly spicy, curry sauce. Variations on the basic *roti* include *roti naan* and *murtabak*.

Other food terms to become familiar with include *mee rebus*, a Malay concoction of noodles, hard-boiled egg and potato, and *hokkien mee*, a tasty dish of noodles incorporating tiny amounts of seafood and meat along with fragments of fried eggs. *Cendol* is an interesting Malay dessert that consists of coconut milk, coloured beans and ice shavings.

Alcoholic drinks are readily available in most restaurants, the only exception tending to be the street cafés serving Muslim food, but the government tax on them is high and this makes them relatively expensive compared to the cost of a meal. Fruit juices prepared from fresh fruit are probably the best-value and healthiest drink to enjoy in Kuala Lumpur. Lime juice goes down well with *roti canai* and sugar cane is often available from mobile stalls by the side of the street. Tea (*teh*) is commonly available as a teabag in a cup, but fresh milk is not always at hand and you may be given condensed milk. But if you're a fan of sweet tea try the local brew, *teh tarik*, which depending on the skill of your host, can involve a theatrical performance of pouring the tea between two cups to froth and cool the mix. There is more choice when it comes to coffee (*kopi*) because you can enjoy a local milky version or go for a cappuccino or latte in one of the hip designer coffee joints along Bukit Bintang or in KLCC.

For information on the wining and dining scene across the whole of Malaysia ⓦ www.dinemalaysia.com focuses on top-end outlets and carries news of current food promotions in the capital.

Entertainment & nightlife

At night, when the noise and density of traffic die down and lights illuminate notable buildings, KL becomes a visually more alluring place. Fairy lights imbue the buildings around Merdeka Square with an attractive quaintness, and this area of the city becomes a lot quieter and more engaging to explore on foot. The glittering Petronas Towers, always a dramatic sight, are quite spellbinding when viewed at night. The streets around Central Market and Petaling Street market have an appeal,

● *Enjoy spectacular views of the city at night*

once the sun goes down, that is not always there during the day – partly because a more leisurely atmosphere prevails and partly because some of the urban shabbiness is lost in the darkness. The stretch of pavement space between Lot 10 and the JW Marriott hotel, known as the Bintang Walk, becomes positively glamorous at night, when neon illuminates the way and the outdoor cafés become, literally, a far cooler place in which to relax with a drink. For a less chic but characterful scene, walk away from the Bintang Walk and down Jalan Bukit Bintang to turn right into Changkat Bukit Bintang. The street life here is more informal, less affluent, but there are still exciting bars like Frangipani (see page 101) to experience.

For more sedate entertainment, check with the **Malaysian Tourism Centre**, also known as MaTic (☎ (03) 9235 4848 ⓦ www.mtc.gov.my) in Jalan Ampang for their schedule of afternoon shows of traditional dance and music, or visit the adjoining Saloma Theatre Restaurant (see page 101). Many of the 5-star hotels have their own nightspots that are open to non-residents, and sometimes the quality of the live music is very good, especially when a Filipino band is in residence.

For performances of classical music, check out what is on at Dewan Filharmonik Petronas (see page 102) on the ground floor of the Petronas Towers. This grand concert hall boasts state-of-the-art acoustic technology; classical music is not always on the programme, but there should be something of interest to music lovers.

Cinemas are plentiful in KL and they usually come in the form of modern cineplexes with programmes that carry Hollywood blockbusters in the original English, as well as

Chinese, Indian and other Asian films, many of which will be subtitled in English. Cinemas usually have the air conditioning turned up high, so it may be worth bringing along a long-sleeved garment or sweater in case it gets a little chilly. In the city centre, the main cinema complexes are in Suria KLCC and Berjaya Times Square. Listings appear in the daily newspapers and on ⓦ www.cinema.com.my and tickets can be booked in advance.

Bars close around midnight and clubs in the city centre have licences that keep them open until 03.00. It is common practice to charge an entrance fee in clubs, but the atmosphere in the bars on Jalan Damaisay and in Bangsar, where entrance charges do not apply, may seem equally if not more amenable to visitors. KL is a fairly safe city, although this is no reason to abandon your 'street smarts' and common sense. Taxis do operate throughout the night although it can be hard to get a 'metered' cab from outside the well-known venues.

For information on what is currently on by way of live music and cultural events generally, check out the Metro section of the *Malay Mail* and advertisements in *The STAR* and *The New Straits Times*. *Juice* magazine is great for information on local happenings and clubbing events, as is online magazine *KLUE* (ⓦ www.klue.com.my). There is no central booking system for events – each establishment has its own booking office.

Sport & relaxation

PARTICIPATION SPORTS

Situated 3 km (2 miles) north of the city, the evocatively named Lake Titiwangsa is a recreational park with a range of activities that includes horse riding, tracks for jogging, tennis and squash courts. To reach it take a taxi or bus 172 from Lebuh Ampang in Chinatown; the bus takes you to Jalan Pahang and from there it is a ten-minute walk to Jalan Kuantan, where the park is situated.

There are a number of golf clubs outside of KL, but all within a day's excursion if you travel by taxi. Two courses that welcome non-members are **The Saujana Golf & Country Club** (ⓐ Saujana Resort Section U2, 40150 Shah Alam ⓣ (03) 7846 1466) and **Bukit Jalil Golf & Country Club** (ⓐ Jalan 3/155B Bukit Jalil ⓣ (03) 8994 1600). Both courses allow non-members to play only on week-days and advance bookings are recommended.

● *Pure luxury in a treatment suite courtyard at Spa Village*

At Port Klang, reachable in around 45 minutes by taxi, the **Royal Selangor Yacht Club** (ⓐ Jalan Shahbandar ⓣ (03) 3168 6964 ⓦ www.rsyc.com.my) runs sailing courses.

RELAXATION

For sport and relaxation in one place, go to Hutan Lipur Kanching (see page 118). Here you can relax by the waterfalls, or head off for the hour-long walk along the signposted path by the first waterfall.

When it comes to finding a green place to relax in and escape the urban sprawl, there is not a lot of choice in the centre of the city. The Lake Gardens (see page 60) are a notable exception.

SPA LIFE
The most luxurious spas are to be found in KL's hotels, but you do not need to be a hotel guest to enjoy the 5-star pampering:

Angsana Spa ⓐ Crowne Plaza Mutiara, Jalan Sultan Ismail
ⓣ (03) 2141 4321 ⓦ www.angsanaspa.com
Anggun Spa ⓐ Hotel Maya, 138 Jalan Ampang
ⓣ (03) 2333 1390 ⓦ www.hotelmaya.com.my
Clark Hatch Spa ⓐ Hilton Hotel, Jalan Stesen Sentral
ⓣ (03) 2264 2830 ⓦ www.clarkhatch.com.my
Sompoton Spa ⓐ Hotel Istana, Jalan Raja Chulan
ⓣ (03) 2148 8910 ⓦ www.thesompotonspa.com
Spa Village ⓐ The Ritz-Carlton, 168 Jalan Imbi
ⓣ (03) 2782 9090 ⓦ www.spavillage.com

Accommodation

Accommodation is available for all budgets, but it is a good idea to have a room booked in advance in KL, at least for the first night or two. Unless you arrive at a particularly busy time, you are unlikely to have difficulty tracking down a place to stay.

Chinatown would be most people's first choice for budget accommodation, but this neighbourhood also includes some good mid-range hotels and is well worth considering as a base for your stay whatever your budget. While Chinatown has the liveliest street life atmosphere, if you want to stay closer to the big shopping malls then the area around Bukit Bintang is best. There is a fair selection of mid-range hotels here. These are rather functional, but bearable if most of your daytime is going to be spent elsewhere. Bukit Bintang, like the area around KLCC, is also home to the top-end, 5-star hotels.

Room rates, apart from those at some hostels, nearly always refer to the cost of the room itself: it makes no difference whether one or two people are occupying it. Having said that, if you are travelling alone you might be able to negotiate a better rate than the one first quoted. Room rates are often more flexible than you think, in all price categories, and if you are staying more than a couple of nights it might be worth suggesting a discount.

PRICE CATEGORIES
The cost of a double room per night including breakfast:
£ up to RM80   ££ RM80–200   £££ over RM200

Many websites, like ⓦ www.asiarooms.com,
ⓦ www.asiahotels.com and ⓦ www.regit.com, take online
bookings, but it can sometimes be worth contacting the hotel
directly to negotiate a better price.

HOTELS

Coliseum £ The most historic hotel in the city and, despite the
fading elegance (and elegance may be going a tad too far), rooms
are still hard to come by here and hard to book in advance. The
street-front rooms undeniably have road noise. Given the colourful
characters that sometimes drop in to the bar downstairs, a single
female traveller might feel more comfortable elsewhere – other
than that, don't hesitate to book it if you want to enjoy a hotel
with character. Clean, tidy rooms as well. ⓐ 100 Jalan Tuanku
Abdul Rahman (Merdeka Square & the Colonial Heritage)
ⓣ (03) 2692 6270 ⓝ Rapid KL Ampang Line: Bandaraya

Ancasa ££ Probably the best place to stay in KL in terms of
balancing comfort and budget considerations. Terrific location
in the heart of Chinatown, with a Rapid KL Transit line station
a couple of minutes away, and excellent facilities for a hotel
with these sorts of room rates. ⓐ Jalan Tun Tan Cheng Lock
(Chinatown) ⓣ (03) 2026 6060 ⓦ www.ancasa-hotel.com
ⓝ Rapid KL Ampang Line: Plaza Rakyat

Bintang Warisan ££ This not-so-posh end of Bukit Bintang has half
a dozen mid-range hotels, but the Bintang Warisan distinguishes
itself from the competition in terms of décor. Friendly service and
good facilities. ⓐ 68 Jalan Bukit Bintang (Bukit Bintang & KLCC)

📞 (03) 2148 8111 🌐 www.bintangwarisanhotel.com Ⓜ KL Monorail: Bukit Bintang

Hotel Malaya ££ A well-established hotel in the heart of Chinatown with old but generally clean rooms with a fridge, television and tea-/coffee-making facilities. Standard rooms have no windows and because of this are very dark, whereas the superior rooms are best for those looking for some natural light. Tours and onward travel can be arranged in the lobby. 📍 Jalan Hang Lekir (Chinatown) 📞 (03) 2072 7722 🌐 www.hotelmalaya.com.my Ⓜ Rapid KL Kelana Jaya Line: Pasar Seni

Hotel Putra ££ One of the few hotels with single rooms. The double rooms come in at the bottom end of the mid-range category. The rooms with a view are well worth it and the lemon walls add a touch of cheer. The money saved in room rates could be devoted to the consumer opportunities in the immediate vicinity. Do note that no food is served on-site so you will need to have breakfast at one of the nearby eateries. 📍 72 Jalan Bukit Bintang (Bukit Bintang & KLCC) 📞 (03) 2141 9228 Ⓜ KL Monorail: Bukit Bintang

Mandarin Pacific ££ Not to be confused with the 5-star Mandarin Oriental. Despite its rundown hallways and slightly tired feel it is, in its own modest way, a decent hotel. It offers comfortable bedrooms with a fridge and safe-deposit box. Laundry service is also available, and there is a coffee shop and a travel agent for arranging city and out of town tours. 📍 2–8 Jalan Sultan (Chinatown) 📞 (03) 2070 3000 🌐 www.mandpac.com.my Ⓜ Rapid KL Kelana Jaya Line: Pasar Seni

Style and comfort at The Westin

Carcosa Seri Negara £££ Renowned, exclusive and expensive hotel set in its own grounds. Once the official residence of Britain's highest representative in colonial Malaya, Carcosa Seri Negara is unique. It's too far to access on foot, so take a taxi from Sentral Station. ⓐ Taman Tasik Perdana (Merdeka Square & the Colonial Heritage) ⓣ (03) 2295 0888 ⓦ www.ghmhotels.com ⓝ Taxi from KL Sentral Station

⬥ *The luxurious lobby of the Hotel Nikko*

Hotel Nikko £££ Superb 5-star hotel and the best place to stay in KLCC. The grand lobby sets the style and there is a fab signature Japanese restaurant as well as an English-style pub; amenities include a fitness centre, spa and hair salon, plus a Chinese restaurant and a brasserie. ⓐ 165 Jalan Ampang (Bukit Bintang & KLCC) ❶ (03) 2161 1111 ⓦ www.hotelnikko.com.my ⓝ Rapid KL Kelana Jaya Line: Ampang Park

JW Marriott £££ A 29-storey, landmark hotel in the city, with Bukit Bintang literally on the doorstep. If shopping and eating are your priorities, then you may never need public transport. ⓐ 183 Jalan Bukit Bintang (Bukit Bintang & KLCC) ❶ (03) 2715 9000 ⓦ www.marriott.com ⓝ KL Monorail: Bukit Bintang

The Westin Kuala Lumpur £££ Great location and a chic, contemporary style make The Westin one of the most stylish places to stay in Kuala Lumpur. Over 400 rooms, but high standards are maintained throughout. The breakfast spread is really incomparable and no other hotel even comes close in this respect. ⓐ 199 Jalan Bukit Bintang (Bukit Bintang & KLCC) ❶ (03) 2731 8333 ⓦ www.westin.com/kualalumpur ⓝ KL Monorail: Bukit Bintang

HOSTELS

Pudu Hostel £ An excellent selection for budget accommodation. Choice of dorm, single, and double rooms, breakfast included, and a bar on the premises, plus laundry, satellite TV and a pool table. Internet available in the same building. ⓐ 3rd Floor, Wisma Lai Choon, 10 Jalan Pudu (Chinatown) ❶ (03) 2078 9600 ⓦ www.puduhostel.com ⓝ Rapid KL Ampang Line: Plaza Rakyat

THE BEST OF KUALA LUMPUR

Trying to fit a lot in on a short stay might seem feasible in theory but the tropical climate, let alone the packed shopping malls, will sap your energy more quickly than you think. Slow down, decide on your priorities and allow time for cold drinks and the leisurely observation of KL life.

TOP 10 ATTRACTIONS

- **The buzz of Bukit Bintang** Stroll down the capital's catwalk in the glare of neon (see page 90)

- **Central Market** Shop for arts and crafts in an art deco building (see page 76)

- **Lake Gardens** A bird park in open parkland and, nearby, the elegant house where British governors resided during the colonial era (see page 60)

- **Masjid Jamek** Escape the urban hubbub by visiting a serene mosque in an oasis of calm (see page 81)

- **Coliseum** Enjoy a meal or drink at the Coliseum while soaking up the authentic atmosphere of KL's historic watering hole (see page 74)

- **Merdeka Square** Step back into history and admire architectural gems of a bygone age (see page 65)

- **Muzium Negara** Get an insight into the diverse cultures of Malaysia at the National Museum (see page 70)

- **A night out in Jalan Doraisamy** Join the late-night partying in a street filled with bars and restaurants (see page 75)

- **Petronas Towers** Visit the tallest buildings of the 20th century, symbol of the country's modernity (see page 94)

- **Temples, tea and t-shirts in Chinatown** Look around the Sri Mahamariamman Temple, shop for bargains in a frenzied street market and, at Cha-No-Yu, savour the refined ritual of Chinese tea-drinking (see page 76)

🔽 *From towers to temples: the best of KL*

Suggested itineraries

HALF-DAY: KUALA LUMPUR IN A HURRY

If you only have a half-day free, arrive early at the Petronas Towers to secure your ticket for a ride to the Skybridge between the towers. Afterwards, at the nearby Suria KLCC, satisfying your upmarket shopping desires will be subject only to your credit card limits, but the enjoyment of local cuisine at the mall's food court will cost very little.

1 DAY: TIME TO SEE A LITTLE MORE

With a day in Kuala Lumpur, you can visit the Petronas Towers, as in the half-day itinerary, then, after some retail therapy at Suria KLCC, take a taxi ride to Merdeka Square to catch glimpses of an older city's architecture. A visit to Chinatown is also a must. You can then spend the rest of your time shopping in Bukit Bintang, or people-watching from an outdoor café on Bintang Walk. If the night is yours, head off to Jalan Doraisamy, where the street is filled with bars and restaurants to satisfy all tastes.

2–3 DAYS: TIME TO SEE MUCH MORE

Spend the first day or so exploring the options suggested above, and then use the extra time to pursue different activities that suit your interests. A visit to the Muzium Negara will occupy half a day, and so would a trip to the Chinese Thean Hou Temple or the Lake Gardens. A walk up Jalan Tuanku Abdul Rahman from Merdeka Square takes in less modern aspects of the city, while an evening reservation at one of the top-drawer restaurants would be a perfect end to the day.

LONGER: ENJOYING KUALA LUMPUR TO THE FULL

A stay of more than three days would allow time for all of the
major attractions to be experienced, and there should also be
time to plan a day out to Batu Caves or even an overnight stay
in Melaka.

⬤ *Enjoy views of the city from the Skybridge*

Something for nothing

While of course the very raison d'être of the good businesspeople of Kuala Lumpur is to separate you from as many ringgits as they possibly can in as pleasurable a fashion as they possibly can, you can still have a wonderful time here without compromising your personal exchequer to any degree. There are no admission charges for the Petronas Towers, Masjid Jamek or Thean Hou Temple. There is a wealth of early 20th-century architecture in and around Merdeka Square that can freely be appreciated by the discerning visitor. The square is an ideal place to start the exploration of these modern architectural delights. The Dayabumi Complex, with its intricate, filigree-like arrangement of what are miniature arches, is not far away. The big draw, of course, are the Petronas Towers, and they are best admired from directly outside and at ground level. Indeed, this is a city that's full of architecture of the very highest order and, your appetite whetted, more of the same can be admired at the PAM Building and EKRAN House. Not far away is the Old Railway Station, another legacy of British rule, and across the road from it is the last Moorish-style building to be erected in the capital, which is open to a free wander.

It is possible to spend money in Chinatown, but equally it costs nothing to soak up the atmosphere, at its best after dark; this is just as true of Bintang Walk. During the day, an interesting walk taking in a face of KL that will eventually fall prey to property developers is along Jalan Tuanku Abdul Rahman. A cup of coffee or a cold drink in one of the street's old-style Muslim cafés or amid the faded elegance of the Coliseum will cost very little and provide a good opportunity to observe the details of KL lifestyle. If you prefer fresh open spaces, head off to the Lake Gardens.

▲ *Merdeka Square gives access to buildings old and new*

When it rains

When it rains, it tends to be a heavy downpour and an umbrella provides minimum cover, so you have little choice but to seek an escape route to somewhere dry. The good news is that such downpours rarely last more than an hour or so – you would be very unlucky to experience a whole morning or afternoon of rain. The chances are, too, that if you are caught out by an unexpected rainstorm or cloudburst, then somewhere not too far away there will be a shopping mall in which to seek shelter. Hotels are another good bet because they all have cafés and/or restaurants, as well as comfortable seating areas, in which to wait out the rain. A taxi for hire always becomes a rarity when it's raining, and the more prolonged the shower the more difficult it is to find an empty vehicle, so hail one as soon as possible if you are caught out and need to get somewhere.

Museums are always useful places to visit during inclement weather and the Muzium Negara (see page 70) has enough exhibition space to occupy the best part of a morning or afternoon. The Central Market (see page 76), a large covered building of two floors, is equally welcoming during wet weather, and as well as all the shops there are cafés and a bar in which to linger until the blue sky reappears or the rain cloud moves on elsewhere.

Temples are another good place to visit in the rain; KL is home to Chinese, Hindu and Buddhist temples. The Chan See Shu Yuen Temple (see page 77) and the Sri Mahamariamman Temple (see page 82) are particularly outstanding.

🔺 *Take shelter in a temple*

On arrival

TIME DIFFERENCE

Kuala Lumpur is eight hours ahead of Greenwich Mean Time all year round, which means it is only seven hours ahead of British Summer Time.

ARRIVING

By air

KLIA (Kuala Lumpur International Airport ☎ 8776 2000 ⓦ www.klia.com.my) is 72 km (46 miles) south of the city at Sepang. The quickest way into the city is by the KLIA Ekspres, a train that operates from Level 1 and which brings you in half an hour, non-stop, into KL Sentral, the main transport hub in Kuala Lumpur; the fare is around RM35. Trains leave every 15 minutes during peak hours (🕑 05.00–09.00, 16.00–22.00) and every 20 minutes at other times. From KL Sentral, taxis can be booked using a pre-pay system or you can take a short walk to the Rapid KL Transit station to access the city train network.

There are airport coaches that depart hourly (🕑 06.30–00.30) from Ground Level, Block C of the Covered Car Park, and arrive at KL Sentral in approximately one hour. For an additional fee, you can buy a ticket that will include a shuttle between KL Sentral and hotels within Chinatown, KLCC, Bukit Bintang and the Golden Triangle area. For details and prices phone ☎ (03) 8787 3895 or consult ⓦ www.airportcoach.com.my

Taxis are pre-paid for at a desk in the arrivals hall; fares average around RM90 into the city centre, including toll charges.

The main terminal for international arrivals is KLIA,

> **TIP**
> If travelling with Malaysian Airlines, Cathay Pacific or Royal
> Brunei, when departing KL you can check in and deposit
> your stored luggage at check-in desks at KL Sentral before
> boarding the KLIA Ekspress to the airport.

however a low-cost carrier terminal, **LCCT** (☎ (03) 8777 8888
ⓦ http://lcct.airasia.com), services Air Asia and Air Asia X flights.
LCCT is located 20 km (12 ½ miles) from KLIA. Shuttle buses run
regularly between KLIA and LCCT.

By rail
If you arrive by train from either Singapore or Thailand, you will
arrive at KL Sentral.

FINDING YOUR FEET
Kuala Lumpur can be a confusing place to orientate oneself
around, partly because there is no obvious centre and partly
because the train transport system is not integrated. Take the
city on an area-by-area basis, beginning with the streets around
your hotel, and see where you are in relation to the nearest
Rapid KL Transit stations.

ORIENTATION
The Bukit Bintang area, formed around the junction of Jalan
Bukit Bintang and Jalan Sultan Ismail, has the most hotels and
shopping malls. Chinatown is the liveliest part of the city and

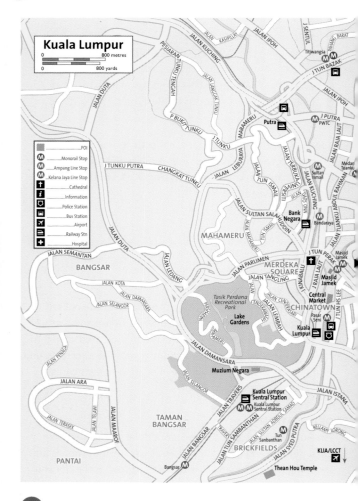

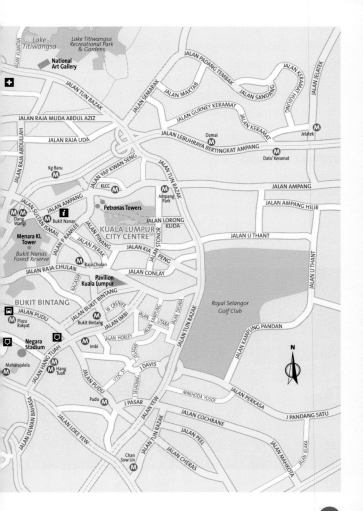

makes the best base for sightseeing. KLCC (Kuala Lumpur City Centre) and Jalan Ampang is an area to the northeast dominated by the Petronas Towers. The area around Merdeka Square was the colonial heart of the city and is rich in architecture, but badly served in terms of restaurants and hotels. To the west of here lie the Lake Gardens, where you can escape from the car fumes and the human traffic.

GETTING AROUND

Due to the heat, humidity and traffic, it is not easy to travel around the city on foot.

The **KLIA** rail system (☎ (03) 2267 8000 ⓦ www.kliaekspres.com) was built to shuttle passengers and airport employees between KLIA airport and KL Sentral. The service consists of the KLIA Ekspres,

🔺 *The KL Monorail will speed you round the city*

a non-stop service that's extremely popular with tourists and business travellers, and the KLIA Transit, which has three stops. **KTM** (☎ (03) 226 71200 🌐 www.ktmb.com.my) is a commuter service linking KL city with the suburbs and destinations further afield such as Port Klang and Seremban.

Rapid KL (☎ (03) 7625 6999 🌐 www.rapidkl.com.my) is the city's light rail system. Its two originally separate lines have been semi-integrated to form Rapid KL. Locals often still refer to the lines by their old names, STAR and PUTRA, so bear this in mind when you ask for public transport information: Rapid KL Ampang Line and Rapid KL Sri Petaling Line were formerly STAR; Rapid KL Kelana Jaya Line was formerly PUTRA. There is also the KL Monorail system, again with its own stations and ticketing procedures, which usefully connects KL Sentral with the Bukit Bintang area.

Trains run from 06.00 to midnight and fares start at 70 sen. Stored tickets (magnetic strip cards) are available for each rail line but can only be used on the particular line that runs from the station you purchased them from. The exceptions are if you buy a monthly Travel Card (which can be used on Rapid KL lines, and on certain bus routes) but this doesn't make financial sense if you are here for a short time. Or, as many of the locals do, you can purchase a Touch N Go card, which can also be used for parking, tolls and the like. It helps to keep a supply of coins ready to hand for ticket machines; otherwise you have to queue up for the counter service.

Officially taxis are supposed to be metered but often many drivers claim traffic congestion or broken meters as reasons for insisting on a 'fixed' and often inflated fare so be ready to practice your negotiating skills or move on to the next taxi. Taxis

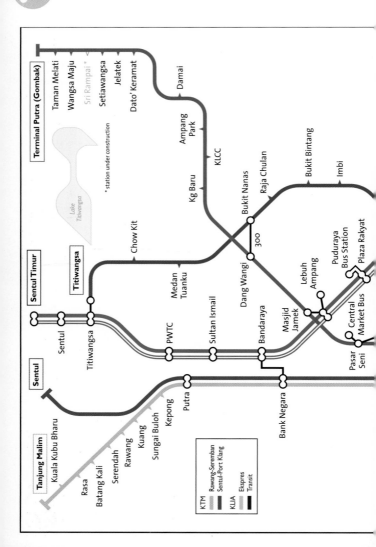

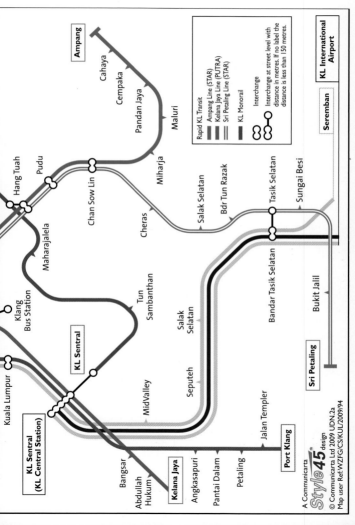

Ampang

Cahaya
Cempaka
Pandan Jaya
Maluri

Hang Tuah
Pudu
Chan Sow Lin
Miharja

Salak Selatan
Bdr Tun Razak

Cheras

Kuala Lumpur

Klang
Bus Station

Maharajalela

KL Sentral

Tun
Sambanthan

MidValley

Seputeh

Salak
Selatan

Tasik Selatan

Sungai Besi

Seremban

Bandar Tasik Selatan

Bukit Jalil

**KL International
Airport**

Bangsar

Abdullah
Hukum

**KL Sentral
(KL Central Station)**

Kelana Jaya

Angkasapuri
Pantai Dalam

Petaling

Jalan Templer

Sri Petaling

Port Klang

Rapid KL Transit
Ampang Line (STAR)
Kelana Jaya Line (PUTRA)
Sri Petaling Line (STAR)
KL Monorail

Interchange

Interchange at street level with
distance in metres. If no label the
distance is less than 150 metres.

A Communicarta
Style 45 design
© Communicarta Ltd 2009 UDN.2a
Map user Ref:WZFG/CSJKUL/2009/94

are usually plentiful, except during rush hours (from 08.00 to 10.00 and 16.30 to 18.30) or during a rain storm, when you can find yourself stuck in traffic jams or at the mercy of the driver's manic manipulation of shortcuts and diversions. Fares start at RM2 and increase 10 sen per 200 m (220 yd), which makes most journeys quite affordable. It is not easy to hail a taxi on the street but taxi stands are dotted around the place and are always to be found outside shopping malls. Long-distance taxis, to Batu Caves for example, are not metered, so you need to agree a fare beforehand.

There are a bewildering number of bus routes, but fares are cheap, around RM1.30 for a journey. They need to be paid in cash as you board the bus; no change is given. Destinations are clearly displayed on the outside of buses.

It is tricky to cover large sections of the city using the public buses as a single journey can involve many changes. For getting around the KL City Centre you would expect to use City Bus (Bandar), which is operated by Rapid KL and Metrobus.

The **KL Hop-on Hop-off city tour** (❶ 1800 88 5546 ⓦ www.myhoponhopoff.com), which stops near all the city's main sights, is useful if you want to get an overview of the city and connect its different areas together. Commentary is available in multiple languages. The double-decker air-conditioned buses provide a bit of relief from the humidity, although their glass roofs sometimes can detract from this on a sunny day. Tickets cost RM38 (for 24 hours) and RM65 (for 48 hours) and can be purchased on the bus or at the many hotels and agents around the city.

❶ *Merdeka Square forms the historic heart of the city*

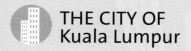
THE CITY OF
Kuala Lumpur

THE CITY

Merdeka Square & the Colonial Heritage

This locale, skirting areas to the west and north of Chinatown, will divide itself up geographically according to your needs. For sightseeing and an appreciation of KL's unique, colonial-era architecture, Merdeka Square should be your destination, a short walk from Masjid Jamek station on the Rapid KL Transit lines. From here, too, you can explore Jalan Tuanku Abdul Rahman. To enjoy time out in the Lake Gardens, take the brief taxi ride from in or around Merdeka Square. For eating, drinking and general entertainment, the focus is Jalan Doraisamy, a short walk from Bandaraya Rapid KL Transit station.

SIGHTS & ATTRACTIONS

Dayabumi Complex

It is worth the easy walk south from Merdeka Square to see at close quarters this brilliant example of modern architecture inspired by forms of Islamic art. From a distance it is difficult to make out the design, but when you are near it the pattern of its motif, tiny arches impossible to count, becomes apparent. At night, it is even more impressive, as lights emphasise its presence.

ⓐ Jalan Sultan Hishamuddin ⓝ Rapid KL Transit Lines: Masjid Jamek

Lake Gardens

The Lake Gardens date back to the 1880s, when they were laid out by the British, and cover 104 hectares (257 acres) of landscaped

🔺 *The Islamic influence is clear in the Dayabumi Complex*

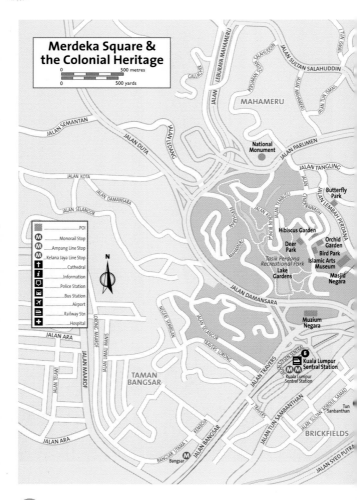

Merdeka Square & the Colonial Heritage

0 _____ 500 metres
0 _____ 500 yards

JALAN SEMANTAN
JALAN DUTA
JALAN LEDANG
JALAN KOTA
JALAN DAMANSABA
JALAN SELANGOR
JALAN ARA
JALAN TELAWI
JALAN MAAROF
JALAN ARA
LORONG MAAROF
SHAW JALAN NIK
NEGRI SEMBILAN
JALAN SELANGOR
JALAN TRAVERS
JALAN TRAVERS
TRAVERS LORONG
JALAN BANGSAR
BANGSAR UTAMA 1
KEMBOJA
JALAN TUN SAMBANTHAN
JALAN SULTAN TORDUL SAMAD
JALAN SYED PUTRA

GALLROS
SALAHUDDIN
JALAN LEBURAYA MAHAMERU
JALAN SULTAN SALAHUDDIN
ARSAM
JALAN MAHAMERU
JALAN TUN ISMAIL
TOR ISMAIL

MAHAMERU

National Monument

JALAN PARLIMEN

JALAN TANGLING

Butterfly Park

JALAN LEMBAH PERDANA

Hibiscus Garden

Orchid Garden

Deer Park

Bird Park

Tasik Perdana Recreational Park

Islamic Arts Museum

Lake Gardens

Masjid Negara

JALAN DAMANSARA

Muzium Negara

STESEN SENTRAL

6 Kuala Lumpur Sentral Station

Kuala Lumpur Sentral Station

Tun Sambanthan

BRICKFIELDS

TAMAN BANGSAR

Bangsar

Legend:

- POI
- Ⓜ Monorail Stop
- Ⓜ Ampang Line Stop
- Ⓜ Kelana Jaya Line Stop
- Cathedral
- ℹ Information
- Police Station
- Bus Station
- Airport
- Railway Stn
- Hospital

N

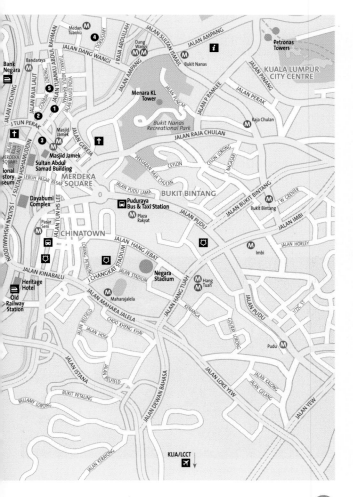

parkland built around an artificial lake. Flower gardens, including a section devoted to orchids, a bird park, a butterfly park and an area for deer all add to the appeal of a visit here. After entering, the National Monument is hard to miss: it is claimed that it is the world's largest freestanding bronze sculpture. Designed by the man who created the Iwo Jima monument in Washington DC, it commemorates those who died fighting communist insurgents in the 1950s, which is ironic in that they were combating nationalists. From the monument, follow the signs for the Butterfly Park, where thousands of them dart around some 15,000 plants. The delightful Hibiscus Garden can be taken in on the way to the Bird Park or to the Deer Park, where the tame animals roam freely. Look out for the kancil, the smallest hoofed animal in the world, otherwise known as the mouse deer. The

⬤ *The flamingo pond in the Lake Gardens Bird Park*

Orchid Garden is not far away, filled with 800 different species.
ⓐ Lake Gardens, Jalan Parlimen **ⓣ** Bird Park (03) 2272 1010;
Butterfly Park (03) 2693 4799 **ⓛ** 09.00–18.30 **ⓝ** Taxi from Masjid
Jamek Rapid KL Transit station or Merdeka Square. Admission
charge for the Bird Park and Butterfly Park

Masjid Negara (National Mosque)

Humidity permitting, you could walk to the National Mosque
from the Lake Gardens or the Old Railway Station; otherwise it
is a short taxi ride. Built in 1956, it occupies a 5 hectare (12 acre)
site and the central prayer hall holds over 10,000 worshippers.
The 18 stars on the summit represent the 13 states of Malaysia
plus the five pillars of Islam. It is best not to visit on a Friday, when
worshippers are making their prayers and the central hall is out
of bounds, but on other days you are free to wander around and
admire the Islamic designs and decorations. As with Masjid Jamek,
shoes must not be worn and robes can be borrowed. The Islamic
Arts Museum (see page 69) is close by. **ⓐ** Jalan Lembah Perdana
ⓣ 2693 7784 **ⓛ** 09.00–12.00, 15.00–16.30, 17.15–18.30 Sat–Thur,
but please note that prayer times – when you may not enter –
vary on a daily basis **ⓝ** Rapid KL Kelana Jaya Line: Pasar Seni
and then a taxi or walk

Merdeka Square

This is the city's historic centre, going back to early colonial
times when the British played cricket on the green lawn, the
Padang, and where independence (*merdeka* in Malay) was
formally declared at midnight on 31 August 1957. The mock-
Tudor building on the western side is the Royal Selangor Club,

founded in 1884 as a social and cricket club for the expatriate community, and once known as the 'Spotted Dog' because of the presence of a pet dog that was frequently tied up outside while its owner sipped gins inside. It remains a highly exclusive, though multiracial, club for KL's privileged class. The nearest place most visitors will find refreshment is in the square's underground complex, Plaza Putra. The National History Museum (see page 71) is very close by. ❸ Merdeka Square, Jalan Raja Laut Ⓝ Rapid KL Transit Lines: Masjid Jamek

Old Railway Station

Until Sentral was built, this was the main railway station, but it now serves commuter lines and the legendary Eastern and Oriental Express. Come here to admire the grandest expression of late Victorian public architecture in southeast Asia. Designed by A B Hubbock, it was completed in 1911, and is unlike any other railway station you are likely to see. Combining Gothic with Moorish influences, with a dose of sheer fantasy added, it is still a remarkable sight. The building across the road was also designed by Hubbock, as the railway's administrative block, and is a good place for taking photographs. The **Heritage Hotel** (❶ (03) 2273 5588 Ⓦ www.heritagehotelmalaysia.com) is worth checking out for its period details, and a drink or snack here is a good excuse to wander about in the hotel where rubber planters from 'up country' would often stay when they arrived in the capital by train. ❸ Jalan Sultan Hishamuddin Ⓝ Rapid KL Kelana Jaya Line: Pasar Seni

Sultan Abdul Samad Building

Standing in Merdeka Square and looking across the road from

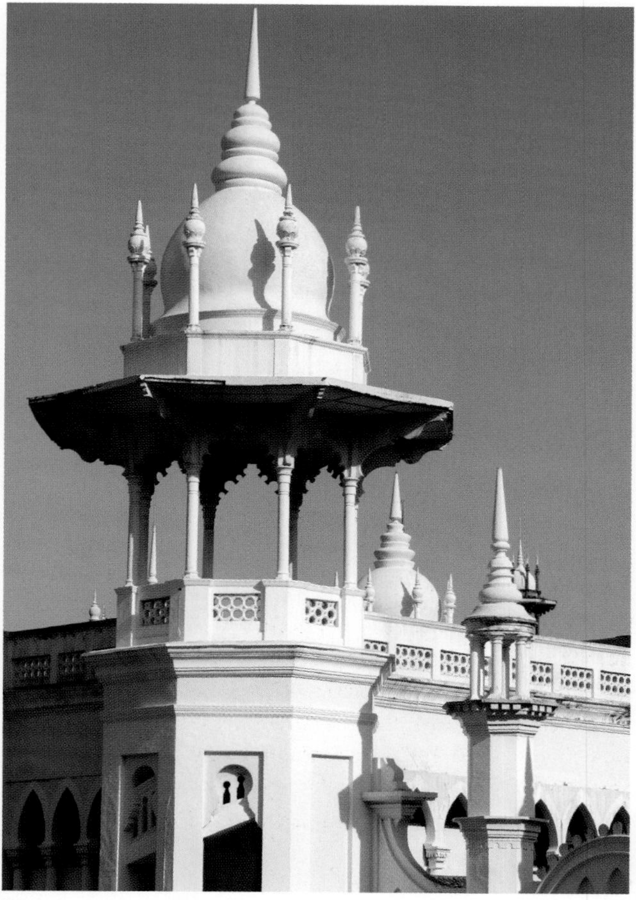

Gothic meets Moorish in the Old Railway Station

⬤ The domes and clock tower of the Sultan Abdul Samad Building

the Royal Selangor Club, the building with a clock tower and copper dome, flanked by two circular towers with their own copper domes, is the Sultan Abdul Samad Building. The stonelike exterior is only a plaster covering over what is an entirely brick-built building, the construction of which began in 1894. It was built to house British government departments, including the Public Works and the Survey Office, and is now home to Malaysia's judiciary. Cross the road to stand under its porch, in order to admire the horseshoe arches and the fine design details, and then take the arched walkway, on the south side of the Sultan Abdul Samad Building, which brings you to the Old Post Office, built between 1904–07. It is similar in style, with an arched verandah and stair towers. The three-storey building on the corner is now the Industrial Court, opened in 1905 as a shopping store. Look for the twin-arched window bay and the oriel windows at the corners. ⓐ Jalan Sultan Hishamuddin ⓝ Rapid KL Transit Lines: Masjid Jamek

CULTURE

Islamic Arts Museum

The design of this museum building, a huge open-plan public space, is itself an expression of Islamic form. There are exhibitions, from all around the Islamic world, of ceramics, metalwork and calligraphy as well as miniature replicas of noted buildings like the Taj Mahal. A good museum shop, and a café. ⓐ Jalan Lembah Perdana ⓣ (03) 2274 2020 ⓦ www.iamm.org.my ⓛ 10.00–16.00 Tues–Sun ⓝ Rapid KL Kelana Jaya Line: Pasar Seni and then a taxi or walk. Admission charge

Muzium Negara (National Museum)

The style of the building is pure Malay, the curving roofs a
characteristic feature of what is called Minangkabu architecture.
Inside, there are interesting exhibitions, which record what was
the traditional lifestyle of the Malay people for centuries but
which is now gradually disappearing. The weaving of ceremonial
cloth, fishing, music, warfare, the matrimonial ceremony and
the role of royalty are well illustrated by way of artifacts and
models. Especially interesting is the section on Peranakan life,
a unique hybrid culture that came about when Chinese male
immigrants married Malay women. ⓐ Jalan Damansara
ⓣ (03) 2282 6255 ⓦ www.muziumnegara.gov.my ⓒ 09.00–18.00
Mon–Fri ⓝ KTM: Sentral. Admission charge

◐ One of the stunning domes at the Islamic Arts Museum

National History Museum

This three-storey 1909 building was constructed to house a
bank and was designed to complement the Mogul style of the
neighbouring colonial buildings, hence the arches and corner
domes. It flooded in 1926 and millions of dollars were laid out
on the *padang* to dry in the sun. A museum since 1996, it houses
a mildly interesting introduction to Malaysia's history. 🅐 29 Jalan
Raja Laut 🅣 (03) 2694 4590 🅦 www.nationalhistorymuseum.gov.my
🕒 09.00–18.00 🅝 Rapid KL Transit Lines: Masjid Jamek

RETAIL THERAPY

Jakel Well regarded department store that bustles with activity
at weekends, when local women flock here to buy the latest fabrics
from Korean silk and French lace to all types of furnishing fabrics.
It's five floors of sheer bliss for any material girl (or guy as there's
also a section dedicated to men's suit fabrics). 🅐 209–212 Wisma
Jakel Jln Bunus, off Jalan Masjid India 🅣 (03) 2698 6798
🕒 10.00–20.00 🅝 Rapid KL Ampang Line: Bandaraya

Rafi Textiles Fabrics from China and Korea, sold by the metre,
and all reasonably priced. The shop can by accessed by heading
through a corridor lined with textile stalls, away from the Coliseum
and up one flight of stairs. 🅐 51, Lot 19–20, Tingkat 1–2 Aked Salihan,
Jalan Tuanku Abdul Rahman 🅣 (03) 2698 7937 🕒 10.00–19.00
🅝 Rapid KL Transit Lines: Masjid Jamek

Razali Batik This store has a good range of batik prints from
the Kota Bahru region, on the northeast coast of Peninsular

Malaysia, as well as cotton and silk garments for men and women. ⓐ Lot B1, Arked Metropoint, 49 Jalan Tuanku Abdul Rahman ⓣ (03) 2691 1350 ⓛ 10.00–18.00 Ⓝ Rapid KL Transit Lines: Masjid Jamek

TAKING A BREAK

Bilal £ ❶ Bilal has been around for 30 years and serves excellent *roti bakar* (toast) and *thosai* (rice flour pancake) for breakfast. Biryani, seafood and *murtabak* (wheat flour pancake or *roti canai* filled with minced meat curry, eggs and onions) are served during the day. At night go for *bubur kacang* (sweet porridge of mung beans and coconut milk). Milkshakes and fresh fruit but no alcohol. ⓐ 37 Jalan Tuanku Abdul Rahman ⓣ (03) 2692 8948 ⓛ 08.00–20.00 Ⓝ Rapid KL Transit Lines: Masjid Jamek

President Café £ ❷ Another typical Muslim coffee shop/restaurant cooking fresh food each day. Convenient for a quick *nasi goring* (fried rice) or *roti canai* or, if a more substantial lunch is required, just point to whatever takes your fancy from the hotplates. ⓐ 28 Jalan Tuanku Abdul Rahman ⓣ (03) 2697 6873 ⓛ 07.00–21.00 Mon–Sat, 07.00–19.00 Sun Ⓝ Rapid KL Transit Lines: Masjid Jamek

Restoran Jamek £ ❸ The quintessential, unpolished Muslim street restaurant, serving *roti canai*, biryani and *murtabak*. Not air conditioned but very convenient for a coffee or a meal after visiting nearby Masjid Jamek. ⓐ 7 Jalan Tun Perak ⓣ 017 684 8624 (mobile) ⓛ 06.30–21.30 Mon–Fri, 07.30–20.30 Sat & Sun Ⓝ Rapid KL Transit Lines: Masjid Jamek

AFTER DARK

RESTAURANTS

CoChine/Bar SaVanh ££ ❹ The place to come for a choice of Cambodian, Laotian or Vietnamese food or to start off your crawl down the charming pub and club district of Asian Heritage Row.

BANGSAR

Bangsar, or Bangsar Baru, is a neighbourhood one stop south of KL Sentral on the Rapid KL Kelana Jaya line. It remains a trendy suburban place to wine and dine, although it does face competition from Desa Sri Hartamas, another emerging hot spot in the suburbs. Reservations are recommended during weekends but during weeknights you can take your pick from the numerous restaurants and bars that are conveniently clustered close to one another. Nearly everywhere falls into the middle price category. **Alexis Bistro** (🅰 29 Jalan Telawi 3 ☏ (03) 2284 2880 🌐 www.alexis.com.my), serving local cuisine but with international touches, competes with **Telawi Street Bistro** (🅰 1 Jalan Telawi 3 ☏ (03) 2284 3168 🌐 www.telawi.com.my/tsb) as the hippest place to eat. For tapas, try **La Bodega** (🅰 14 & 16 Jalan Telawi 2 ☏ (03) 2287 8318 🌐 www.bodega.com.my/labodega). For drinks before or after a meal there is **The Social** (🅰 57 & 59 Jalan Telawi 3 ☏ (03) 2282 2260 🌐 www.thesocial.com.my), which is characterised by loud music and pool tables.

> **THAT LAST MEAL**
> If you are leaving for the airport from Sentral station, you could do worse than allow time for a final meal of distinction. The Hilton Hotel is only a walk away and at Senses restaurant (see opposite) you could enjoy a memorable evening meal.

In this part restaurant, part bar and part café, the meals are light and oh-so-tasty and the zen-like interior is enough to induce a meditative state, never mind the drinks. ⓐ 64 Jalan Doraismy ⓣ (03) 2697 1180 ⓦ www.indochine.com.my ⓛ CoChine Lounge & Restaurant: 18.30–22.30 Mon–Thur, 18.30–23.30 Fri & Sat; CoChine Café: 12.00–23.00 Mon–Fri, 17.00–23.00 Sat; Bar SaVanh: 17.00–01.00 Mon–Thur, 17.00–03.00 Fri & Sat ⓝ KL Monorail: Medan Tuanku

Coliseum ££ ❺ Unprepossessing from the outside, this is one of the capital's most historic eating places, a favourite haunt of expatriate rubber planters during the 1950s and retaining some of the atmosphere of those times. The place still manages to bring in the local crowd for lunch, serving a mix of Asian and Western food, but suits those looking for a reminder of the past rather than culinary excellence. It's worth stopping in here for a cold beverage and a slightly quirky experience. A good drinks list, including cocktails. ⓐ 98 Jalan Tuanku Abdul Rahman ⓣ (03) 2692 6270 ⓛ 10.00–22.00 ⓝ Rapid KL Ampang Line: Bandaraya

Senses £££ ❻ Malaysia's most renowned chef, Cheong Liew, is the consultant to Senses, and it shows in a dazzlingly imaginative menu that includes star treats such as barramundi and prawn sushi, *wagyu* sirloin, and scallops and goat's cheese with a beetroot sauce. Modern Australian cuisine is the focus, as is the elegant setting. The white Irish linen tablecloths and gleaming silverware enhance the dining experience. **⊜** Hilton Hotel, Jalan Stesen Sentral **☎** (03) 2264 2264 **ⓦ** www.kl-studio.com **🕐** 12.00–14.30, 19.00–22.30 Mon–Fri, 19.00–22.30 Sat **Ⓝ** KTM: Sentral

BARS & CLUBS

Al's @ Heritage Kick back and sip on a glass of wine while you watch the action on Jalan Doraisamy unfold. Al's doesn't promise the lively atmosphere that some other pubs lay claim to, instead its ethos is simply: chill out. **⊜** 26 Jalan Doraisamy **☎** (03) 2692 0992 **🕐** 12.00–15.00, 18.00–23.00 Mon–Thur, 12.00–03.00 Fri, 18.00–03.00 Sat, 18.00–23.00 Sun **Ⓝ** KL Monorail: Medan Tuanku

Mojo DJs spin tunes from Wednesday to Saturday. There are five pool tables upstairs, while downstairs is usually packed with revellers on their way to or from one of the many restaurants on Jalan Doraisamy. **⊜** 42 Jalan Doraisamy **☎** (03) 2697 7999 **🕐** 11.00–03.00 **Ⓝ** KL Monorail: Medan Tuanku

Chinatown

Chinatown is the area of KL that every visitor needs to experience, and not just in terms of trying to bag a bargain in the street market. It is the neighbourhood where the cultural and commercial pulse of the city beats most insistently. There is a lot to see. The shopping scene is not glitzy because there are no giant shopping malls, and there is no equivalent to the glamour of Bintang Walk, but Chinatown is where you finally get the opportunity to experience a real sense of Asia – and in a city where Chinese culture is strong but not predominant and where other races also assert their identity and their traditions.

SIGHTS & ATTRACTIONS

Central Market

This attractive, brightly painted art deco building from the 1930s, originally the city's wet (live animal) market, was closed down in the 1980s and renovated to form what is now one of the best places to stroll around, indulge in some low-key shopping and enjoy a drink or meal in one of the food establishments. There is some tourist schlock, but you will also find some interesting shops, with craft goods from Borneo and Indonesia and, especially at weekends, some form of musical entertainment in the pedestrianised area outside the market. ⓐ Jalan Hang Kasturi ⓣ (03) 2274 6542 ⓦ www.centralmarket.com.my ⓛ 10.00–21.00 ⓝ Rapid KL Kelana Jaya Line: Pasar Seni

Chan See Shu Yuen Temple

If you want to experience a more traditional side to Chinatown than that expressed by the night market, take an early morning walk down the streets parallel to Jalan Petaling. There are unreconstructed buildings that date back to the early decades of the 20th century and traditional coffee shops where you should venture in and try one of the breakfasts; just ask for what someone else is eating and rest assured that it will cost so little that it won't matter if it turns out not to be to your taste. At the southern end of Jalan Petaling, Chan See Shu Yuen Temple will

◗ *The night market at Jalan Petaling*

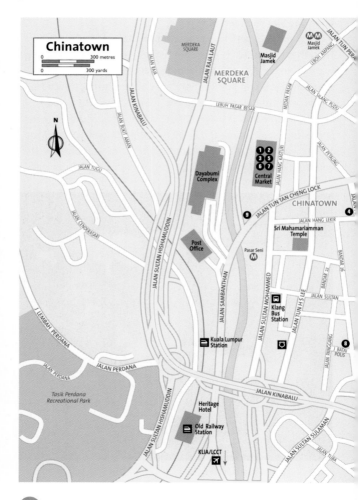

0   300 metres
0   300 yards

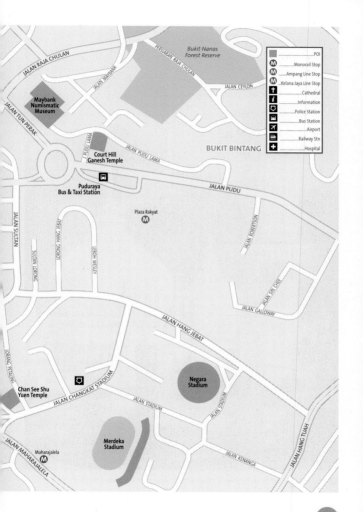

◆ *The delightful Masjid Jamek, the oldest mosque in Kuala Lumpur*

have its share of devotees standing or kneeling before the colourful statues of different deities. The chief one here is Chong Wah, a Sung Dynasty emperor, but he competes for space with representations of dragons and various other creatures fighting determined-looking warriors. 🅐 172 Jalan Petaling 🅣 (03) 239 6511 🅛 08.00–19.00 Ⓝ KL Monorail: Maharajalela

Jalan Petaling

Vastly overrated as a place to shop, this is still worth visiting just to experience the frenzied ambience and see the vast array of counterfeit goods that lure in visitors. Not for the fainthearted or the claustrophobic, the atmosphere is everything, though make sure you keep your wallet or purse in a place safe from pickpockets. This is the place to engage in some light-hearted banter with the vendors and maybe make the occasional purchase of something you don't really need. 🅛 Night market 18.00–22.30 Ⓝ Rapid KL Kelana Jaya Line: Pasar Seni

Masjid Jamek

The location of Masjid Jamek is a historic spot: it was exactly here, at the confluence of the rivers Gombak and Klang, that a group of Chinese tin miners decided to make a camp in 1857. In doing so, they were unknowingly founding Malaysia's capital, because the camp drew in more miners and a settlement rapidly developed. It is not surprising, then, that the street where the mosque stands also marks the northern end of Chinatown.

Masjid Jamek is the oldest mosque still standing in the city. It was built in 1909, and it retains a great deal of charm for this reason. The architect was A B Hubbock, the man responsible for the Old Railway Station and other buildings, and his Indian-inspired penchant for Mogul design features is equally apparent in the form of this pretty mosque. Despite the hustle and bustle of the modern city a mere couple of hundred metres away, there is always a sense of peace and quiet about Masjid Jamek and it is very relaxing to walk around the place. The central prayer hall is topped by three domes, minarets seem to be everywhere and small palm trees help sustain the mood that most visitors welcome when stepping into Masjid Jamek and away from the roaring traffic. ⓐ Jalan Tun Perak ① (03) 2691 2829 ① 08.00–13.30, 14.30–18.00 ⓝ Rapid KL Transit Lines: Masjid Jamek

Sri Mahamariamman Temple

The most photogenic temple in Chinatown is a Hindu one, the Sri Mahamariamman. It was built in the 1870s by Tamils, who left India in the hope of finding work on the new railways being built by the British on the Malay Peninsula. The ornately decorated gate tower, the *gopuram*, is the most eye-catching feature of the temple, and this dates back to the 1960s, when the fading original was renovated. The tower is decorated with more than 200 statues of Hindu gods and stands 23 m (75 ft) high. It is from this temple that the procession to Batu Caves (see page 116) starts each year at the festival of Thaipusam, and the statue of Lord Murugan, the centrepiece of the procession, is housed inside. ⓐ 163 Jalan Tun H S Lee ① (03) 3238 3647 ① 06.00–20.30 ⓝ Rapid KL Kelana Jaya Line: Pasar Seni ① The temple is under renovation until 2010. It will remain open but parts of it may be covered in scaffolding during this time

COURT HILL GANESH TEMPLE

This little Indian temple is often missed by visitors, tucked away as it is, off Jalan Tun Tan Cheng Lock. Look for the Pudu Hostel on Jalan Pudu and turn up the small street here, Jalan Pudu Lama, to find the temple 100 m (110 yd) up on the right side. It always seems to be busy with devotees because it occupies such a small amount of space, and it serves as a reminder that Chinatown also has its Indian community. Stalls outside are constantly busy making and selling garlands and incense sticks for the worship of Lord Ganesh, a statue of whom is visible inside the temple. ⓐ Jalan Pudu Lama ⓒ 08.30–18.00 Ⓝ Rapid KL Ampang Line: Plaza Rakyat

CULTURE

Maybank Numismatic Museum

A visit here could conveniently follow a trip to the nearby Court Hill Ganesh Temple but, unless you have a particular interest in coins, the Numismatic Museum is probably not worth a journey of its own. Having said that, the building is a fine example of modern Islamic architecture and it is worth seeing close up. The exhibits in the museum cover the whole history of monetary exchange, starting with cowrie shells and covering the early history of the Malay Sultanates. The colonial period is represented as well, and so too are the years of Japanese occupation during World War II. Other unique exhibits are the coins that were

The stunning gate tower of the Sri Mahamariamman Temple

produced by the tin and rubber companies for their employees during the late 19th century.

There is a food and drink centre on the same floor – it is actually for Maybank employees but visitors are welcome to use it. ⓐ 1st Floor Maybank Building, 100 Jalan Tun Perak ☎ (03) 2070 8833 🕐 10.00–16.30 Mon–Fri Ⓜ Rapid KL Ampang Line: Plaza Rakyat

RETAIL THERAPY

Arch Collection A small art gallery filled mostly with appealing photographs of KL taken by a local photographer. A good spot to shop for an easy-to-pack souvenir or gift. ⓐ 1.07A, Ground Floor, Central Market ☎ (03) 2072 0832 🕐 10.00–21.00 Ⓜ Rapid KL Kelana Jaya Line: Pasar Seni

Bukit Nusantara Malaysian batik for women and men in the form of shirts, blouses, pants and scarves. Fabric can also be purchased in lengths of 2.5 m and 4 m (8 ft and 13 ft). This is one of the better-quality shops in Central Market. ⓐ M20, 1st Floor, Central Market ☎ (03) 2273 2277 🕐 09.00–22.00 Ⓜ Rapid KL Kelana Jaya Line: Pasar Seni

Jalan Petaling Now covered with a glass ceiling for all-weather shopping, the stalls in this market start appearing by mid-afternoon and by dusk the place is beginning to fill with punters; after dark, it is heaving with visitors expecting bargains. If your bargaining skills are working well you may pick up some t-shirts, belts, DVDs or fake designer watches and handbags at reasonable prices, but do not come expecting anything by way of quality merchandise. ◗ Night market: 18.00–22.30 Ⓝ Rapid KL Kelana Jaya Line: Pasar Seni

Mombai Touch Not just Indian crafts, there is plenty here from Borneo as well, and a nice selection of Malaysian-produced fabrics as well as embroidered cloth from India. The shawls and scarves are some of the best quality to be found in Kuala Lumpur. ⓐ KB1 & KB2, Ground Floor, Central Market ⓣ (03) 2273 7619 ◗ 10.00–21.00 Ⓝ Rapid KL Kelana Jaya Line: Pasar Seni

Native Galaxy Gallery An Aladdin's Cave of arts and crafts from Borneo, especially Sarawak, as well as Thailand and Indonesia. You should expect a discount of around 10 per cent off the prices; packaging and shipping can be arranged for large items but there is plenty here that will squeeze into your luggage. ⓐ 10–12 Jalan Hang Lekir ⓣ (03) 2070 4567 ◗ 10.30–20.00 Ⓝ Rapid KL Kelana Jaya Line: Pasar Seni

Purple Cane Tea Art Centre A modern take on the traditional tea shop with a huge range of stock. ⓐ 11 Jalan Sultan ⓣ (03) 2031 1877 Ⓦ www.purplecane.com.my ◗ 10.00–22.00 Ⓝ Rapid KL Kelana Jaya Line: Pasar Seni

Warisan Craft Warisan Craft is packed with wooden crafts from Sarawak and Sabah, mostly mock weapons and masks, but also a selection of jewellery that includes some attractive agate rings. ⓐ BB 14–16 Lorong Melayu, Central Market ⓣ 017 385 7128 (mobile) ◗ 10.30–21.00 Ⓝ Rapid KL Kelana Jaya Line: Pasar Seni

TAKING A BREAK

Central Market Food Court £ ❶ Stroll around and consider the food options from different regions of Asia including Thai, Nonya and Malaysian fare. Renovated to resemble the feel of a shophouse, booths overlook the market area. ❷ Gallery Level, Central Market ☎ (03) 2273 7389 ⏱ 10.00–21.00 Ⓝ Rapid KL Kelana Jaya Line: Pasar Seni

Malay Tea House £ ❷ Tucked away in the back of Central Market is this cosy respite joint that focuses on Malay teas prepared from fresh herbs – a healthy alternative to a mug of froth indeed. Malay tea is believed to improve all kinds of ailments, from arthritis to colds and flus. ❷ KB 14 15 16 Lorong Melayu, Central Market ☎ 017 300 7811 (mobile) ⏱ 10.00–21.00 Ⓝ Rapid KL Kelana Jaya Line: Pasar Seni

Old Town Kopitiam £ ❸ Marble-top tables character to the place and there is a good choice of snacks – the Kaya toast is worth a bite – and light meals like curries and *Ipoh hor fun* (flat rice noodles). ❷ Ground Floor, Central Market ☎ (03) 2273 1278 ⏱ 10.00–21.30 Ⓝ Rapid KL Kelana Jaya Line: Pasar Seni

Restoran Kim Lian Kee £ ❹ *Hokkien Mee* (soy-coated yellow noodles mixed with prawns, pork and squid) is the staple for many who dine here. This coffee shop has a fine reputation that's totally deserved. ❷ 49–51 Jalan Petaling (opposite Hong Leong Bank) ☎ (03) 2032 4984 ⏱ 11.00–23.00 Ⓝ Rapid KL Kelana Jaya Line: Pasar Seni

THE CITY

Secret Recipe £ ❺ Secret Recipe does a range of goodies throughout the day. The outlet in Central Market is only one of many; others are to be found in Bukit Bintang, Lot 10, Suria KLCC and other locations around the city. ❸ Ground Floor, Central Market ❶ (03) 2274 6824 ❽ www.secretrecipe.com.my ❹ 09.00–21.30 ❻ Rapid KL Kelana Jaya Line: Pasar Seni

Ginger £–££ ❻ Lime walls brighten this dimly lit interior and when the food arrives, it will lift your spirits even more. Ginger serves all the usual Thai favourites as well as Indonesian and Malay fare. This is a great option if you are looking for a restaurant experience rather than a simple food court. ❸ M12, Central Market ❶ (03) 2273 7371 ❹ 11.30–21.30 ❻ Rapid KL Kelana Jaya Line: Pasar Seni

Precious Old China Restaurant & Bar £–££ ❼ Not as homely and characterful as the Old China Café (see below), although under the same management and with a similar style, this is still a pleasant retreat from the outdoor heat and the crowds within Central Market. Draught beer, wine, teas and juices and a wider choice of Nonya dishes than the smaller sister restaurant can offer. ❸ M2, Central Market ❶ (03) 2273 7372 ❹ 11.30–21.30 ❻ Rapid KL Kelana Jaya Line: Pasar Seni

AFTER DARK

Old China Café £ ❽ In the heart of Chinatown, yet away from the hustle and bustle, this charmingly decorated restaurant evokes the Baba-Nonya community of Melaka and Penang.

There are old photographs to study and the marble-top tables you eat from are originals from old Chinese coffee shops. Come here at lunchtime for a one-dish meal like *nasi lemak* or *nyonya laksa* and you may be tempted to return in the evening when the atmosphere is at its best. Excellent menu, with suggested meals for anyone new to Chinese cuisine. ⓐ 11 Jalan Batai Polis ① (03) 2072 5915 ⓦ www.oldchina.com.my ② 11.30–22.00 ⓝ Rapid KL Kelana Jaya Line: Pasar Seni

Restoran Hameed £ ❶ Very easy to find once you step out of Pasar Seni station, this is a good spot for a quiet, inexpensive meal in the evening. North Indian and Malay curries are cooked daily. ⓐ 21 Jalan Tun Tan Cheng Lock ② 24 hours ⓝ Rapid KL Kelana Jaya Line: Pasar Seni

BARS & CLUBS

The Beatles Bar If it's been a hard day's night haggling at Petaling Street, pop into The Beatles Bar and you could easily imagine you're anywhere but Chinatown. ⓐ 143 Jalan Tun HS Lee ① (03) 2072 1834 ② 17.00–03.00 ⓝ Rapid KL Kelana Jaya Line: Pasar Seni

Reggae Bar A DJ gets going around 19.00, and from then on the music is loud – and, yes, Bob Marley is frequently played. There are pool tables for the quieter hours; spirits cost less for women but the beer, sold by the glass or jug, is the same price for all customers. Live music at weekends. There's even a guesthouse attached. ⓐ 158, Ground Floor, Jalan Tun H S Lee ① (03) 2026 7960 ⓦ www.reggaebarkl.com.my ② 12.00–02.30 Mon–Sat, 15.00–02.30 Sun ⓝ Rapid KL Kelana Jaya Line: Pasar Seni

Bukit Bintang & KLCC

Bukit Bintang and KLCC are both dense with restaurants and bars, to suit all but the most spartan budgets, and Bukit Bintang is a particularly good hunting ground for entertainment after dark. During the day, its dense cluster of shopping malls could keep you as busy as your bank balance allows. KLCC, apart from being a huge shopping centre, is next door to the Petronas Towers, the number-one attraction in the city.

SIGHTS & ATTRACTIONS

Bintang Walk

Touted, a tad ambitiously, as KL's answer to Paris's Champs Elysées and Tokyo's Ginza rolled into one, this stretch of Jalan Bukit Bintang between Lot 10 and KL Plaza is a hip place to stroll down at night. You can also enjoy an iced coffee, a beer or a meal at one of the many alfresco cafés. During the day, giant air-conditioning units blast out cold air so even on the pavement it never gets uncomfortably hot. ❷ Jalan Bukit Bintang Ⓝ KL Monorail: Bukit Bintang

Bukit Nanas Forest Reserve

Only a few steps away from Menara KL, the Bukit Nanas Forest Reserve offers a surprising patch of tropical greenery, nearly 10 hectares (25 acres) in size, with forest trails and abundant flora and fauna. The 45-minute forest tour introduces you to Malaysia's indigenous rubber tree and there is a good chance of spotting macaque monkeys hopping about the trees, plus

◆ *The Menara KL towers above the city*

THE CITY

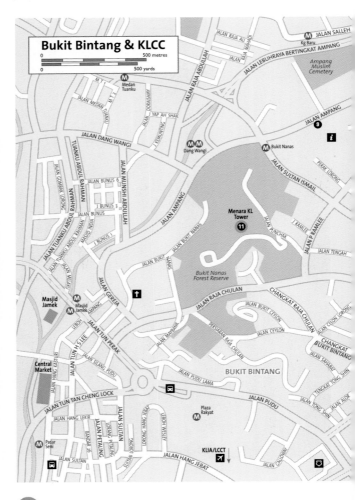

Bukit Bintang & KLCC

0 — 500 metres
0 — 500 yards

JALAN RAJA ALI HADI
JALAN SALLEH
Kg Baru
JALAN
JALAN LEBUHRAYA BERTINGKAT AMPANG
Ampang Muslim Cemetery
Medan Tuanku
JALAN MEDAN TUANKU
JALAN DORAISAMY
JALAN YAP AH SHAK
JALAN KAMUNTING
JALAN RAJA ABDULLAH
JALAN AMPANG
JALAN DANG WANGI
Dang Wangi
Bukit Nanas
i
TUANKU ABDUL RAHMAN
JALAN BUNUS 6
J BUNUS 3
JALAN MUNSHI ABDULLAH
JALAN SULTAN ISMAIL
JALAN CONLAY LORONG
JALAN TUANKU ABDUL RAHMAN
JALAN BUNUS
MASJID INDIA
JALAN AMPANG
Menara KL Tower
11
J RAMLEE
JALAN P RAMLEE
J BUNUS
JALAN TUANKU ABDUL RAHMAN
JALAN NINU
JALAN BUKIT NANAS
JALAN PUNCHAK
JALAN TENGAH
JALAN GEREJA
JALAN BUKIT NANAS
Bukit Nanas Forest Reserve
Masjid Jamek
Masjid Jamek
JALAN TUN PERAK
JALAN RAJA CHULAN
CHANGKAT RAJA CHULAN
JALAN BUKIT CEYLON
JALAN CEYLON LORONG
JALAN TUN H S LEE
JALAN MARBUK
PERSIARAN RAJA CHULAN
JALAN CEYLON
CHANGKAT BUKIT BINTANG
JALAN SAHABAT
Central Market
JALAN HANG KASTURI
JALAN TUN H S LEE
JALAN SILANG PUDU
JALAN PUDU LAMA
BUKIT BINTANG
TENGKAT TONG SHIN
JALAN ALOR
JALAN TUN TAN CHENG LOCK
Plaza Rakyat
JALAN PUDU
JALAN YONG SHIN
JALAN HANG LEKIR
JALAN SULTAN
JALAN PETALING
LORONG HANG JEBAT
LEBOH WESLEY
JALAN GALLOWAY
Pasar Seni
BANDAR 35
LORONG PETALING
SULTAN
KLIA/LCCT
JALAN SULTAN
JALAN HANG JEBAT

9

92

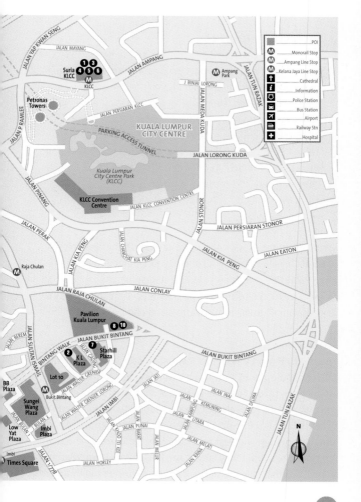

	POI
Ⓜ	Monorail Stop
Ⓜ	Ampang Line Stop
Ⓜ	Kelana Jaya Line Stop
✝	Cathedral
🛈	Information
☆	Police Station
🚌	Bus Station
✈	Airport
🚆	Railway Stn
✚	Hospital

JALAN MAYANG

JALAN YAP KWAN SENG

JALAN AMPANG

Suria KLCC
❶ ❸
❹ ❺ ❻
Ⓜ KLCC

Petronas Towers

Ampang Park Ⓜ

J BINJAI LORONG

JALAN MEDA KUDA

JALAN TUN RAZAK

JALAN P RAMLEE

JALAN PERSIARAN KLCC

KUALA LUMPUR CITY CENTRE

PARKING ACCESS TUNNEL

Kuala Lumpur City Centre Park (KLCC)

JALAN LORONG KUDA

JALAN PINANG

KLCC Convention Centre

JALAN KLCC CONVENTION CENTRE

JALAN STONOR

JALAN PERSIARAN STONOR

JALAN PERAK

JALAN KIA PENG

JALAN CHANGKAT KIA PENG

JALAN KIA PENG

JALAN EATON

Raja Chulan Ⓜ

JALAN RAJA CHULAN

JALAN CONLAY

Pavilion Kuala Lumpur
❽ ❿

JALAN BEREM

JALAN SULTAN ISMAIL

BINTANG WALK

JALAN BUKIT BINTANG

❼

❷ K L Plaza

Starhill Plaza

JALAN CADING

Lot 10

JALAN BUKIT BINTANG

JALAN WALTER GRENIER

Bukit Bintang

BB Plaza

JALAN WALTER GRENIER LORONG

JALAN IMBI

JALAN ATI

JALAN INAI

JALAN KEMUNING

JALAN DELIMA

JALAN TUN RAZAK

Sungei Wang Plaza

JALAN PUDU

JALAN PUDU 2

Low Yat Plaza

Imbi Plaza

JALAN IMBI

JALAN KHOO TIE KEE

JALAN PUNAI

JALAN UTARA

JALAN MELUR

JALAN MELATI

JALAN RAJA ALI

Imbi
Times Square

JALAN 1/77B

JALAN HORLEY

N

93

MENARA KL TOWER

The viewing platform of the Menara KL is higher even than that of the Petronas Towers, so you will get a spectacular view of the city and the twin towers themselves that cannot be beaten. There is a revolving restaurant if you fancy dining up in the clouds (see page 101). Completed in 1994, this communications tower is still one of the tallest in the world. Be prepared for queues. ⓐ Jalan Punchak, off Jalan P Ramlee ⓣ (03) 2020 5444 ⓦ www.menarakl.com.my ⓛ 09.00–22.00 ⓡ KL Monorail: Bukit Nanas. Admission charge

some of the thousands of species of insects that live in this natural oasis in the heart of the city. ⓐ 12 Jalan Punchak, off Jalan P Ramlee ⓣ Bukit Nanas Forest Reserve: (03) 2034 2609 ⓦ www.menarakl.com.my ⓛ 08.00–18.00 (last tour at 16.30) ⓡ KL Monorail: Bukit Nanas. Admission charge

Petronas Towers

The twin, 88-storey Petronas Towers constituted the world's tallest building until Taiwan's 101 Building edged a bit higher. Visitors can take a free ride to the viewing platform between the 41st and 42nd levels, but places are limited, and when the ticket office on the concourse level opens at 08.30 there is often already a queue. The best exterior, close-up views of the towers are from the attractively landscaped KLCC Park immediately in front. From the park, it is difficult not to be impressed by architect

Cesar Pelli's achievement, and the labour of 7,000 people in making 65,000 sq m (700,000 sq ft) of stainless steel into something so aesthetically pleasing. At night, the park's two water fountains light up and dance to the sound of music. ⓐ KLCC, Jalan Ampang ⓣ (03) 2331 1769 ⓦ www.petronastwintowers.com.my ⓛ 09.00–19.00 Tues–Thur, Sat & Sun, 09.00–13.00, 14.30–19.00 Fri ⓝ Rapid KL Kelana Jaya Line: KLCC

RETAIL THERAPY

BB Plaza Come here for the two anchor tenants, Metrojaya and Tangs, both mid-range department stores. The other shops here are the usual mix of fashion outlets, home décor, shoes and handbags. ⓐ Jalan Bukit Bintang ⓣ (03) 2148 7411 ⓛ 11.00–21.30 ⓝ KL Monorail: Bukit Bintang

Lot 10 Pricewise, Lot 10 is a notch or two up from Sungei Wang Plaza but not at the luxury-boutique level of Starhill Gallery, which is further down Jalan Bukit Bintang. Lot 10's anchor tenant is the Isetan department store, while the various outlets tend to be brand-name ones like Guess, Timberland and British India. ⓐ Jalan Sultan Ismail ⓣ (03) 2141 0500 ⓛ 10.00–21.30 ⓝ KL Monorail: Bukit Bintang

Mng Clothes and accessories from Barcelona and very stylish too. Mng also has an outlet in the Isetan department store in Lot 10. ⓐ C46, Concourse Level, Suria KLCC, Jalan Ampang ⓣ (03) 2163 3198 ⓛ 10.00–22.00 ⓝ Rapid KL Kelana Jaya Line: KLCC

Pavillion Kuala Lumpur Since opening in 2008, this light and contemporary mall has become popular for its multitude of eateries, from restaurants to an all-encompassing food court. While the centre does focus on luxury goods, it is also home to more 'down to earth' stores such as Zara, Quiksilver and Topshop. If you're looking for an air-conditioned retreat without emptying your wallet, you'll also find a large bookstore with a café and a cinema. **ⓐ** 168 Jalan Bukit Bintang **ⓣ** (03) 2118 8833 **ⓦ** www.pavilion-kl.com **ⓛ** 10.00–22.00 **ⓜ** KL Monorail: Bukit Bintang

Petronas Towers Gift Shop No prizes for guessing what is on sale here: images of the towers in every format and material you could imagine – jigsaw, metal, illuminated, pewter, printed

● *Buy a souvenir at the Petronas Towers*

on cards, posters and t-shirts. ⓐ Concourse Level, Petronas Towers, KLCC, Jalan Ampang ⓣ (03) 2331 1744 ⓛ 09.00–19.00 Tues–Sun, 09.00–17.00 Mon ⓝ Rapid KL Kelana Jaya Line: KLCC

Regain Invoking the Chinese saying that the aging process begins from the foot, Regain's foot reflexology treatments may hold out the promise of rejuvenation but, in the meantime, they should relieve tired feet after an extended shopping trawl through Bukit Bintang's shopping plazas. ⓐ D-4, Ground Floor, KL Plaza, 179 Jalan Bukit Bintang ⓣ (03) 2148 3500 ⓛ 12.00–00.00 ⓝ KL Monorail: Bukit Bintang

Royal Selangor Silver and gold jewellery and decorative items for the home, like photograph frames, chess and mahjong sets. ⓐ 118, Level 1 Ramlee Mall, Suria KLCC, Jalan Ampang ⓣ (03) 2382 0240 ⓦ www.royalselangor.com. ⓛ 12.00–22.00 ⓝ Rapid KL Kelana Jaya Line: KLCC

Saw Prices and style can be compared with the other hairdresser in Suria KLCC – Fusion Salon next door – but Saw is considered to have the edge, so to speak. ⓐ Lot 401, Ampang Mall, Suria KLCC, Jalan Ampang ⓣ (03) 2171 1881 ⓦ www.saw.com.my ⓛ 10.00–22.00 ⓝ Rapid KL Kelana Jaya Line: KLCC

Sungei Wang Plaza With over 500 shops, this is probably the best mid-range consumer mall in the city. Claustrophobic at weekends, so it is best to arrive early on a weekday for a more stress-free experience. Sungei Wang is especially good for clothes, opticians and, on the third floor, electronics. ⓐ Jalan Sultan Ismail

📞 (03) 2148 6109 🌐 www.sungeiwang.com 🕐 10.00–22.00
🔵 KL Monorail: Bukit Bintang

Suria KLCC A vast consumer centre where you could spend an entire day shopping, eating and being entertained. Most types of shopping are accommodated here in one of four interconnected malls: Ampang, Park, Ramlee and Centre Court. This is not budget

🔺 *Shopping heaven at Suria KLCC*

shopping, so don't expect to get bargains here. The post office located in the mall is open daily until 18.00. See page 131 for the Aquaria and page 102 for the cinema complex. ⓐ Jalan Ampang ⓣ (03) 2382 3326 ⓦ www.suriaklcc.com.my ⓛ 10.00–22.00 Ⓝ Rapid KL Kelana Jaya Line: KLCC

TAKING A BREAK

Little Penang Kafé £ ❶ A terrific place for a tasty lunch. Try one of the set meals like the five-spice chicken or the prawn or beef curry. If you're after a thirst-quencher, go for ice *kacang* – shaved ice with syrup, milk, red beans, *attap* seeds and banana slices. ⓐ 409, 4th Floor, Suria KLCC ⓣ (03) 2163 0215 ⓛ 11.30–15.30, 16.30–21.15 Ⓝ Rapid KL Kelana Jaya Line: KLCC

Moussandra £ ❷ The selection of set lunches on the menu, competitively priced for this part of town, makes this Mediterranean-style restaurant worth a visit. Expect pizzas, pasta and tapas. ⓐ B8 Mezzanine Level, KL Plaza, Jalan Bukit Bintang ⓣ (03) 2144 0775 ⓦ www.moussandra.com ⓛ 12.00–15.00, 18.00–23.00 Ⓝ KL Monorail: Bukit Bintang

Rasa £ ❸ There are two food centres in Suria KLCC. The other one, Signature's, is on the second level of Park Mall, while Rasa is on the fourth level of Ampang Mall. Most of the outlets serve Malay food, but Tom Yam is Thai and there are some others doing Western and Asian favourites. ⓐ 4th Floor, Ampang Mall, Suria KLCC ⓣ (03) 2382 0224 ⓦ www.suriaklcc.com.my ⓛ 07.00–22.00 Ⓝ Rapid KL Kelana Jaya Line: KLCC

Al-Marjan Café £–££ ❹ This is the café section of the Al-Marjan restaurant (see below), which has small tables outside, from where you can look down on the flow of consumers on the various levels below. Good coffees and Oriental-style sandwiches. ⓐ 415, 4th Floor, Suria KLCC ⓣ (03) 2168 8557 ⓛ 12.00–22.00 Ⓝ Rapid KL Kelana Jaya Line: KLCC

AFTER DARK

RESTAURANTS

Al-Marjan Restaurant ££ ❺ Lebanese and Iranian cuisine with some delectable appetisers to enjoy in preparation for a spicy lamb or other meat dish served in the Middle East style. ⓐ 415, 4th Floor, Suria KLCC ⓣ (03) 2168 8557 ⓛ 12.00–22.00 Ⓝ Rapid KL Kelana Jaya Line: KLCC

Chakri Palace ££ ❻ Promoted as Royal Thai cuisine, it is the décor more than the cuisine that evokes royal luxury, but there is some interesting food on the menu. ⓐ 417, 4th Floor, Ramlee Mall, Suria KLCC ⓣ (03) 2382 0887 ⓦ www.chakri.com.my ⓛ 12.00–22.00 Ⓝ Rapid KL Kelana Jaya Line: KLCC

My Thai ££ ❼ Authentic Thai cooking and amazing toilets. ⓐ Lower Ground Floor, Starhill Gallery, 181 Jalan Bukit Bintang ⓣ (03) 2148 6151 ⓛ 12.00–00.00 Ⓝ KL Monorail: Bukit Bintang

Prego ££ ❽ The attraction of Prego could be the alfresco scene, though the indoor dining area is comfortably air conditioned, and there are wood-fired pizzas and 13 types of pasta dishes on the menu. ⓐ The Westin Kuala Lumpur, 199 Jalan Bukit Bintang ⓣ (03) 2731 8333 ⓦ www.starwoodhotels.com/westin ⓛ 12.00–14.30, 18.30–22.30; Champagne brunch: 11.30–14.30 Sun ⓝ KL Monorail: Bukit Bintang

Saloma Theatre Restaurant ££ ➒ Located within the grounds of the Malaysia Tourism Centre, the show that accompanies the buffet of Malay food is a one-hour performance of cultural dance and music. ⓐ 139 Jalan Ampang ⓣ (03) 2161 0122 ⓦ www.saloma.com.my ⓛ 19.00–23.00 ⓝ KL Monorail: Bukit Nanas, Rapid KL Kelana Jaya Line: Dang Wangi

Eest £££ ➓ Pan-Asian treats that rise far above the confusion of fusion: very dark, very cool – not to be missed. ⓐ The Westin Kuala Lumpur, 199 Jalan Bukit Bintang ⓣ (03) 2773 8017 ⓛ 12.00–14.30, 18.30–22.30 ⓝ KL Monorail: Bukit Bintang

Seri Angkasa £££ ⓫ The highest restaurant in Malaysia, perched on top of Menara KL, the city telecoms tower. The buffet food is definitely not the best reason for coming here, but if you want amazing views of the city at night, then this is the place to be. ⓐ Menara KL, Jalan Punchak, off Jalan P Ramlee ⓣ (03) 2145 1833 ⓦ www.serimelayu.com ⓛ 12.00–15.00, 19.00–23.00 ⓝ KL Monorail: Bukit Nanas

BARS & CLUBS
Frangipani One of the best bars in the Bukit Bintang area of town. Come here to catch some exciting music and a cocktail. There's also a great French restaurant attached. ⓐ 25 Changkat

Bukit Bintang ☎ (03) 2776 2390 ⓦ www.frangipani.com.my
🕐 18.00–01.00 Tues–Thur & Sun, 18.00–03.00 Fri & Sat
Ⓜ KL Monorail: Bukit Bintang

Zouk Uber-hip Zouk is back in business after undergoing a massive renovation. It's where the beautiful people like to flaunt their chic threads, so dress to impress if you're heading out to this hot – yet cool – dance club. ⓐ 113 Jalan Ampang ☎ (03) 2171 1997 ⓦ www.zoukclub.com.my 🕐 21.00–03.00

CINEMAS & THEATRES

Dewan Filharmonik Petronas The Malaysian Philharmonic Orchestra may not be the world's top ensemble, but the venue is a dramatic one and the acoustics are state of the art. ⓐ Level 2, Tower 2, Petronas Towers, KLCC, Jalan Ampang ☎ (03) 2051 7007 ⓦ www.malaysianphilharmonic.com 🕐 10.00–18.00 Mon–Sat (until 21.00 on concert nights) Ⓜ Rapid KL Kelana Jaya Line: KLCC

Tanjong Golden Village This 12-screen cinema complex in Suria KLCC offers the latest Hollywood blockbusters. Tickets can be booked in advance and this may be necessary at weekends. ⓐ Level 3, Park Mall, Suria KLCC, Jalan Ampang ☎ (03) 7492 2929 ⓦ www.tgv.com.my 🕐 11.00–20.00 Ⓜ Rapid KL Kelana Jaya Line: KLCC

▶ *The main square in Melaka*

Melaka

Melaka, once known as Malacca, is less than two hours away by bus to the south of KL, so a day trip is feasible, although an overnight stay would make the whole trip more relaxing. A visit is worthwhile because the town still has a laid-back, sleepy character that contrasts markedly with KL, and the history of Melaka means there is plenty to see by way of interesting sights. Melaka's sheltered location, halfway between India and China, turned it into an important trading post. The first Europeans to arrive were the Portuguese in the 16th century, followed by the Dutch in the 17th century and finally the British. All this has brought a rich architectural heritage. There is also an unspoiled Chinatown as well as good places in which to enjoy the multi-cultural cuisines of Malaysia. The area of town where the sights and attractions are located is small enough to get around on foot. The local tourist office, on Jalan Kota in the centre of town, is undergoing seemingly endless renovation, but there's a temporary version at the **main bus station** (ⓐ Melaka Sentral Bus Station, Jalan Tun Razak ⓣ (06) 288 1340 ⓦ www.melaka.gov.my).

GETTING THERE

Transnasional (ⓘ 1300 888 582 ⓦ www.transnasional.com.my) is one of Malaysia's major bus companies that's popular with tourists. In addition to their standard bus, Transnasional offers a 'skyview' coach – which boasts ergonomic seating and bigger windows – eight times a day on the Melaka route. Buses depart half-hourly from 08.00–20.00 for the 144 km (93 mile) journey to Melaka from **Puduraya Bus Station** in KL (☎ (03) 2070 3300). The bus station in Melaka is outside the centre of town, but taxis are plentiful and a ride to the main sights or your hotel should cost around RM10. Tours can also be arranged through Ping Anchorage (see page 116), departing at 09.30, either for the whole day or with the option of an overnight stay.

SIGHTS & ATTRACTIONS

Bukit China

In the northeast of town, you can walk to Bukit China (China Hill) by taking Jalan Bukit China to the 18th-century Poh San Teng Temple at the foot of the hill. Close by the temple is the Sultan's Well, built in the 15th century by Sultan Mansor Shah, who married the daughter of a Chinese emperor. The well was fought over many times in the centuries that followed because

● *Bustling Chinatown remains unspoiled*

of its dependable spring. From the temple, head up to what is one of the largest Chinese cemeteries outside of China. The oldest grave dates back to 1688 – you pass it on the way to the summit. Town residents use the hill as a recreational area for jogging, so the place is not as spooky as a cemetery housing 12,000 graves might be.

Chinatown

A short walk across the river from the tourist office, the main street in Chinatown, Jalan Tun Tan Cheng Lock, is the first turning on the left. This is the best-preserved part of what in the 19th century was the town's thriving Chinese quarter. The town houses along this street were the homes of Baba-Nonya families, the result of marriages between wealthy Chinese entrepreneurs – faced with a dearth of Chinese women in the land they had emigrated to – and local Malay women. To find out more about these mixed marriages, visit the Baba-Nonya Museum at numbers 48–50 on the street (see page 110). Ⓐ Jalan Tun Tan Cheng Lock

Christ Church

This mid-18th-century building was a Dutch Reformed Church when it was constructed to mark the centenary of the Dutch arrival in Melaka. But the British converted it into an Anglican place of worship when they added the bell. Its pink bricks were imported from Holland before being faced with local red laterite, giving it a flamboyant appearance that contrasts with the calm, whitewashed interior. The pews are the original ones and each of the roof beams was cut from a single giant tree. The memorials and plaques on the walls tell tales of premature deaths of

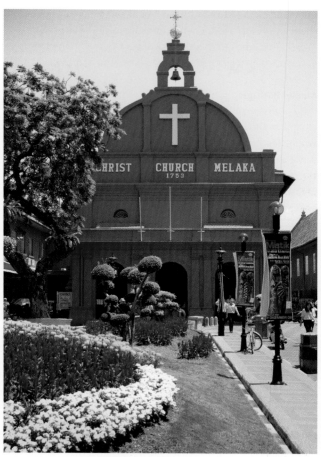

⬥ *The distinctive red frontage of Christ Church*

European expatriates and, a short way to the east of the church, there is an old graveyard with tombstones of Dutch and British inhabitants who also never made it back to their homelands.
ⓐ Town Square ⓣ (06) 282 4510 ⓛ 09.00–17.00

Medan Portugis

Only 3 km (1 ¾ miles) east of the town centre, but too far to walk in the heat, Medan Portugis (Portuguese Square) is where descendants of Melaka's Portuguese settlers live. There is not a lot to see but the seaside location is refreshing and the restaurants try their best to evoke a Eurasian atmosphere.
ⓐ Jalan Albuquerque ⓝ Bus 17 from Jalan Parameswara

Stadthuys (Town Hall)

This is one of the most historic buildings in Melaka, and certainly the most attractive from an architectural point of view. It was constructed as a Town Hall by the Dutch between 1641 and 1660 and its style would not be out of place in a cobbled town square in Holland. Massive wooden doors, thick walls built of brick and gorgeous red in colour, Stadthuys stands proud in what was the heart of the town's Dutch quarter. It houses the Museum of Ethnography (see opposite). ⓐ Town Square ⓣ (06) 284 1934
ⓛ 09.00–17.30 Mon–Thu, 09.00–21.00 Fri–Sun. Admission charge

CULTURE

Baba-Nonya Museum

The building itself constitutes an important part of this museum, being a carefully preserved set of Peranakan houses that were

MARITIME MUSEUM

Next to the river is a reconstruction of the Portuguese ship, the *Flora de la Mar*, and inside you can see the kind of cargo of spices that ships like this carried from the East back to Europe. Across the road, there is the related Royal Malaysian Navy Museum where the most interesting exhibits are items salvaged from the wreck of the *Diana*, which in 1817 sank in shallow water off the coast. ⓐ Jalan Quayside ⓣ (06) 283 0926 ⓛ 09.00–17.30 Mon–Thur, 09.00–21.00 Fri–Sun. Admission charge

built in 1896. True to the Chinese-Malay mix that defines Peranakan, the building features roof tiles from China and ornately carved shutters and doors that are a characteristic feature of Malay domestic architecture. Inside, the museum preserves many examples of everyday Peranakan life, a wealthy lifestyle that could afford heavy blackwood furniture and lacquer screens from China. ⓐ 48–50 Jalan Tun Tan Cheng Lock ⓣ (06) 283 1273 ⓛ 10.00–12.30, 14.00–16.30. Admission charge

Museum of Ethnography

An excellent museum, packed with information on the history of Melaka and the various cultures that made up the town's ethnic mix. This is the place to get your head around Peranakan culture, a unique way of life that evolved from marriages between Chinese immigrants and Malay women. ⓐ Stadthuys, Town Square ⓣ (06) 282 6526 ⓛ 09.00–17.30. Admission charge

RETAIL THERAPY

Mahkota Parade Mahkota Parade is a giant shopping mall, dominated by a Parkson Grand department store. This one-stop store has everything you need, including fast food and a supermarket, and for quality clothes at fixed prices there is nowhere better in Melaka. ⓐ 1 Jalan Merdeka ⓣ (06) 282 6151 ⓦ www.hektargroup.com/mahkotaparade ⓛ 10.00–22.00 Sun–Thur, 10.00–22.30 Fri & Sat

Malaqa House Melaka is famous for its antique shops. However, this reputation is now a little overblown because most of the genuine old stuff was bought up long ago and what you see

⬥ *Seek out antiques in Melaka's famed shops*

now is likely to require some serious renovation work. You would also need to arrange shipping and pay import charges. Malaqa House, on the other hand, offers expensive but beautiful craft items that would fit into your luggage. **ⓐ** 70 Jalan Tun Cheng Lock **ⓣ** (06) 281 4770 **ⓛ** 10.00–17.30

Orangutan House One of the better shops in Melaka selling paintings and arty t-shirts with highly original designs; a good place to browse for a gift. **ⓐ** 59 Lorong Hang Jelat **ⓣ** (06) 2882 6872 **ⓦ** www.charlescham.com **ⓛ** 10.00–18.00

TAKING A BREAK

Farmosa Chicken Rice Ball £ Here you can try chicken rice balls, a local delicacy inspired by Hainanese chicken rice, and mix it up with one of the pork or curry dishes on offer. **ⓐ** 28–30 Jalan Hang Kasturi **ⓣ** (06) 286 0121 **ⓛ** 09.30–21.30

Geographer Café £ The name and style of this eatery draw in travellers seeking the intrepid explorer experience. A good range of local and Western dishes, plus internet access and occasional live music at night. **ⓐ** 83 Jalan Hang Jebat **ⓣ** (06) 281 6813 **ⓛ** 09.00–23.00

Heeren House £ Comfortable café offering ice cream and apple pie during the day, and decent lunches which often feature Peranakan dishes. It also has rooms (see page 115). **ⓐ** 1 Jalan Tun Tan Cheng Lock **ⓣ** (06) 281 4241 **ⓦ** www.heerenhouse.com **ⓛ** 07.30–17.00

Selvam £ Popular banana leaf Indian eatery where tasty curries, vegetarian and meat, are cooked daily. Excellent for breakfast or lunch. ⓐ Corner of Jalan Bandaraya and Jalan Temenggong ⓣ (06) 281 9223 ⓛ 07.00–22.00

AFTER DARK

Capitol Satay £ An inexpensive café where the speciality is *satay cekup*, a mixture of meat and vegetables on a stick that you cook by dipping into a very hot satay sauce. ⓐ 41 Lorong Bukit China ⓣ (06) 283 5508 ⓛ 17.00–00.00 Tues–Sun

Restoran de Lisbon ££ A little out of town, 3 km (1¾ miles) away on the coast, the neighbourhood of Medan Portugis has its Eurasian roots in the meeting of the Portuguese with Malays; the food reflects this cultural mix to some extent. The chilli crabs are a favourite dish. ⓐ Medan Portugis ⓣ (06) 283 5578 ⓛ 12.00–00.00 Tues–Sun

Seri Nyonya ££ A lovely restaurant that evokes Peranakan culture in both its décor and cuisine and which amply compensates for its hotel setting. The Peranakan dessert spread is a particular treat and prices are very reasonable given the standard of service and quality of the food. ⓐ Hotel Equatorial, Jalan Bandar Hilir ⓣ (06) 282 8333 ⓦ www.equatorial.com ⓛ 12.00–14.00, 18.30–22.00

ACCOMMODATION

Eastern Heritage Guest House £ A well located old Peranakan building that retains a rustic charm. It houses a lounge and bar, but for breakfast, you'll have to go elsewhere. ⓐ 8 Jalan Bukit China ⓣ (06) 283 3026

Aldy Hotel ££ A smart, mid-range hotel with a decent café; best of all, all the main attractions are just minutes away on foot. ⓐ Jalan Kota ⓣ (06) 283 3232 ⓦ www.aldyhotel.com.my

Heeren House ££ Terrific location in the Chinatown area and well-kept, tidy rooms in a smart little hotel with an attractive café (see page 113) at street level; breakfast is included in the room rates. ⓐ 1 Jalan Tun Tan Cheng Lock ⓣ (06) 281 4241 ⓦ www.heerenhouse.com

Hotel Equatorial £££ A fine hotel with an excellent range of restaurants and facilities, plus large bedrooms. Room rates should be obtainable at the bottom end of this price category, making a 5-star hotel experience less expensive that you might expect. ⓐ Jalan Bandar Hilir ⓣ (06) 282 8333 ⓦ www.equatorial.com

Around Kuala Lumpur

There are a number of sights and attractions that can be found outside Kuala Lumpur, chief of which is Batu Caves, to the north of the city. A half-day could be spent visiting the caves and then a further stop made at the Orang Asli Museum. The main attraction to the south of KL is Thean Hou Temple.

GETTING THERE

Information on how to reach the various sights and attractions is given separately below; one travel company in KL that covers most of them in its tours is **Ping Anchorage** (ⓐ 27A Jalan Wawasan Ampang 2/1 Bandar Baru Ampang ⓣ 4280 8030 ⓦ www.pinganchorage.com.my ⓛ 09.00–18.00 Mon–Fri, 09.00–13.30 Sat). Most of the sights can be reached by public transport, but getting to some, like the Orang Asli Museum, requires private transport, and it is a matter of taking a taxi from KL or using a tour company. If you arrange your own taxi, agree on the fare and time schedule beforehand. Taxis are plentiful at Batu Caves and you could travel there by bus, see the caves and then hire a taxi for the journey back to the city, detouring via the Orang Asli Museum. Thean Hou Temple can be reached by bus but the taxi ride is a short one and saves a lot of time.

SIGHTS & ATTRACTIONS

Batu Caves
Batu Caves, a large limestone outcrop 13 km (8 miles) north of

Stepping out: Batu Caves

KL, were discovered by accident by an exploring naturalist in the early 1880s. They became a place of worship for Hindus, a shrine to Lord Subramanian was constructed, and gradually the caves became sacred to devotees. Throughout the year, there is a steady stream of visitors, as many motivated by curiosity as religion. Hinduism does not spring to mind when you first arrive and see the large statue of the Buddha, but this changes dramatically during the festival of Thaipusam in February. Then, hundreds of thousands of Hindus flock to Batu Caves and penitents arrive on foot from Sri Mahamariamman Temple in KL (see page 82), wearing metal frames, called *kavadis*, attached to their skin. The penitents walk behind a huge, brightly painted chariot that carries a statue of Lord Murugan (also known as Lord Subramaniam). It is an amazing sight but unless you are happy being part of a million-strong audience, it would be better to view the procession leaving KL.

The main cave, 100 m (330 ft) high and 75 m (250 ft) long, is reached via 273 steps. At the top you stand at the entrance to a dark and dingy-looking place that is enlivened by a small number of colourful statues and the opportunity to have your photo taken next to a giant monitor lizard. Venture inside, getting accustomed to the dark and the pushy monkeys, and make your way through to the rear; a small circle of rock and trees, with light making its way through from above, marks the end of your route. ☎ (03) 6189 6284 ⏰ 06.30–20.30 🚌 Bus: 11 or 69 from Central Market

Hutan Lipur Kanching (Kanching Recreational Forest)
A lovely waterfall walk is the chief attraction of a visit to

🔺 *A watery wonderland at Hutan Lipur Kanching*

Kanching Recreational Forest, 20 km (12 ½ miles) northwest
of KL. The guided path to the waterfall area of Hutan Lipur
Kanching is an uphill walk but there are a number of stopping
places with benches and at one of them there is a pool suitable
for swimming. You do not need any special walking gear but
sandals are inappropriate, especially if it has been raining,
and a sturdy pair of trainers would be best. There is a food stall
near the entrance, but consider bringing some picnic food and,
of course, lots of water. If your visit occurs during the time of
school holidays – from the end of May to the middle of June,
the middle of August and from mid-November to the end of
December – there is a risk that the forest will be overrun by
a large party of noisy schoolchildren. At any time of year,
avoid weekends unless you like a crowd.

It takes about 20 minutes to walk from the waterfall area to
Templer's Park, named after the last British high commissioner,
Sir Gerald Templer. This is sometimes confused with Hutan Lipur
Kanching, but it is not really worth a visit. ➌ Hutan Lipur Kanchung,
Tambang ➊ (03) 6091 6131 ➌ 08.00–20.30 ➌ Bus: Len Omnibus
66, 72 or 83 from Puduraya Bus Station, every hour; last bus back
to KL departs at 20.00; purchase your return ticket from the
forest office

Thean Hou Temple

A hilltop situation for a grand Chinese temple to the south of the
city that was opened in 1989, dedicated to the Taoist goddess
Thean Hou, a water spirit who protects those at sea. Despite
its modernity, the temple adheres to tradition in its design and
the first thing you notice are the bright red pillars and the tiered

● *The delightful Thean Hou Temple*

roof. Inside, there is a colourful display of lanterns and images of swirling dragons.

If you come at weekends you may witness a marriage; the photogenic backdrop is a favourite with young couples and there is a registry office on the premises. You may also see worshippers shaking rattling canisters until a stick falls out to the ground. The number on the stick refers to a numbered piece of paper, which is duly collected from the rack, with the person's fortune conveniently printed for them to read. There is a garden to the rear of the temple, with more statues of deities and a carved set of the 12 animals that make up the Chinese cycle of years.

🅐 65 Pesiaran Indah, off Jalan Syed Putra ☎ (03) 2274 7088
🕐 08.00–21.30 Ⓝ Bus: 27 or 52 from Klang bus station

Zoo Negara

Situated 14 km (8 ¾ miles) northeast of the city centre, Malaysia's National Zoo is home to an ape centre, monkey area and African savannah. The carnivore enclosure is where you'll find the Malayan tiger. Choose between walking or taking the slow train. 🅐 Hulu Kelang, Ampang ☎ (03) 4108 3422 🕐 09.00–17.00 Ⓝ Bus: 170 from Lebuh Ampang. Admission charge

CULTURE

National Art Gallery

The gallery's permanent collections of contemporary Malaysian art occupy the upper two levels; what you see on the lower levels will be the temporary exhibition that happens to be in town at the time of your visit. These can be more engaging, because very little information is provided about the permanent works of art. On the first Saturday of every month there is an arts and crafts fair in the vicinity of the gallery, with products for sale, demonstrations by local artists and live entertainment. The attractive park surrounding Lake Titiwangsa (see map pages 52–3) is a short walk away and boats can be hired here. Or it is enjoyable simply to stroll through the landscaped grounds and see coffee bushes, cashew trees and other indigenous fruit trees. ⓐ 2 Jalan Temerloh, off Jalan Tun Razak ⓣ (03) 4025 4990 ⓦ www.artgallery.gov.my ⓛ 10.00–18.00 ⓝ Rapid KL Bus 114 from KLCC, then a three-to-five-minute walk

Orang Asli Museum

This museum, devoted to the culture of the original inhabitants of the Malay Peninsula, is 25 km (15 ½ miles) north of KL, and with no public transport it is necessary to take a taxi or join a tour. Ping Anchorage's tours to Batu Caves (see page 116) usually include a visit to the museum after the caves. The museum is well organised, with sections devoted to nearly all aspects of Orang Asli culture, and there are lots of authentic exhibits on show. You will see examples of the cane blowpipes used for hunting and the poison that is made from a particular tree. The use of rattan for a variety of purposes is particularly well represented, and there are also displays relating to wedding rituals, fishing techniques and clothes and costumes. Orang Asli sculptures, carved from wood, are highly imaginative versions of fantastic spirits and there are some good examples on show. ⓐ KM 24 Jalan Pahang, Gombak ⓣ (03) 6189 2122 ⓦ www.jheoa.gov.my ⓛ 09.00–17.00 Sat–Thur

⬥ *The museum provides a fascinating glimpse into Orang Asli culture*

THE ORANG ASLI

There are about 50,000 Orang Asli still living in remote areas of Malaysia. Judging by the government's treatment of the nomadic Penan people in Sarawak, it seems likely to be only a matter of time before most of them are integrated into mainstream life. Traditionally, they are nomadic hunters living in a forest environment and creating temporary homes before moving on to a new hunting area. Their tools, canoes for travelling on rivers, cooking implements and hunting weapons are nearly all made from forest materials, though nowadays there is some trade with settled communities for items like cooking pots and t-shirts.

RETAIL THERAPY

Geetha's Rumah Batek This fixed-price, supermarket-sized craft shop sells masks, fabrics, gift and souvenir items from Malaysia. If you want the ultimate in Batu Caves memorabilia, however, check out the battery-lit, framed images of Ganesh the elephant god – only available from the stall at the entrance to the main cave at the top of the 273 steps. ⓐ Sri Supramaniam Swamy Temple, Batu Caves ⓣ (03) 6189 9797 ⓛ 08.30–19.00

Lucky Star Cash & Carry You'll find all things bold and gold here, especially in the form of statues and souvenirs. There's also a selection of embroidered Indian saris and bangles. ⓐ 14, 15 & 16 Kuil, Batu Caves ⓣ (03) 6187 2787 ⓛ 08.00–17.00

TAKING A BREAK

Dhivya's Café £ Snacks are available here, as well as more substantial dishes. As with all the eateries at Batu Caves, vegetarian eating is the order of the day and you will not find any meat-based dishes. ⓐ Shop no. 9, Batu Caves ⓣ (03) 6185 3788 ⓛ 07.30–19.00

Restoran Rani £ This restaurant has the best choice of food at Batu Caves and, for carnivores that have to think they are eating meat, there are mock meat dishes of fish and mutton, using tofu to create what looks like the real thing. The photo-based menu makes it easy to choose and there are lots of visual delights by way of the pyramid-shaped *roti canai*. Try the ginger tea with *thosai* for an authentic Indian vegetarian repast. ⓐ Shop no. 10 Batu Caves ⓣ (03) 6186 2518 ⓛ 07.00–21.30

Nelayan Titiwangsa ££ If visiting the National Art Gallery or Lake Titiwangsa, there are a number of inexpensive hawker stalls in the park; but for something more formal, and in more comfortable, air-conditioned surroundings, try this seafood restaurant floating on a wooden platform in the water. The food is a mixture of Chinese and Malay dishes. ⓐ Jalan Pahang, Lake Titiwangsa ⓣ (03) 4022 8400 ⓦ www.nelayan.com.my ⓛ 12.30–14.30, 18.30–22.30

▶ *KLIA, Kuala Lumpur's international airport*

Directory

GETTING THERE
By air

Flying is likely to be the most convenient method of getting to Kuala Lumpur from other destinations, but you could also arrive by train from Thailand in the north or from Singapore in the south. If travelling between Europe or the USA and Asia, Australia or New Zealand, your airline may offer the choice of a stopover at KL. If KL is your main destination, it is possible to get a flight via most major airlines from European capitals, and from the USA, Australia and New Zealand. Direct flights reduce the journey time from the UK to around 12–13 hours. The number of hours added on to an indirect flight will depend on where you stop and for how long. While the cheapest flights usually entail at least one, lengthy stop, low cost carrier **Air Asia** (Ⓦ www.airasia.com) have defied tradition with the launch of a 13–hour non-stop route between London Stansted and Kuala Lumpur.

Airlines flying to Kuala Lumpur include:

British Airways/Qantas ❶ 1 800 88 1260
Cathay Pacific ❶ (03) 2035 2777
Emirates ❶ (03) 2058 5888
Eva Airways ❶ (03) 2162 2981
KLM/Air France ❶ (03) 7712 4555/**Flying Blue** (03) 6207 4021
Malaysia Airlines ❶ (03) 7843 3000
Singapore Airlines ❶ (03) 2692 3122

Many people are aware that air travel emits CO_2, which contributes to climate change. You may be interested in the possibility of lessening the environmental impact of your flight through **Climate Care** (ⓦ www.climatecare.org), which offsets your CO_2 by funding environmental projects around the world.

By rail

Trains run daily between Bangkok in Thailand, stopping at KL and Singapore. For details see ⓦ www.ktmb.com.my or www.railway.co.th. For general information on train routes to KL see the *Thomas Cook Overseas Timetable* ☎ (01733) 416477 ⓦ www.thomascookpublishing.com

ENTRY FORMALITIES

Visitors of most nationalities are granted a visa upon arrival for a 30-day stay and no payment is required. Make sure your passport has at least six months' validity remaining.
Immigration department ⓦ www.imi.gov.my

CUSTOMS

The duty-free allowance on entering Malaysia is 200 cigarettes and one litre of alcohol. Passengers are prohibited from carrying more than 10,000 USD or foreign currency equivalent and must declare any local currency that exceeds RM1000.

MONEY

The Malaysian currency is the ringgit (RM) and banknotes come in RM2, RM5, RM10, RM20, RM50 and RM100. The ringgit is divided into 100 sen and coins come in 1, 5, 10, 20 and 50 sen pieces, and RM1. For current exchange rates see ⓦ www.xe.com.

Currency can be exchanged in banks and exchange offices, but the easiest way to obtain Malaysian money is by using the

ATM machines which are found at the airport and outside banks. They are easy to locate and screen prompts are usually available in English. There are limits on how much can be withdrawn on any one day, so it makes sense to bring more than one bank debit card, some cash in your home currency and/or, as a backup, some Thomas Cook or American Express traveller's cheques in US dollars, sterling or euros. Credit cards are readily accepted in many hotels, shops and restaurants. For security reasons, never lose visual contact with your card and, if possible, use cash instead.

HEALTH, SAFETY & CRIME

There are no compulsory vaccinations, but your doctor may advise inoculation against Hepatitis A and B, tetanus and typhoid.

Tap water is safe for brushing teeth, but for drinking it is best to use the bottled water that is available everywhere in the city. Should you suffer from a mild stomach complaint or diarrhoea, pharmacies sell standard treatments and oral rehydration salts. Pharmacies have English-speaking staff and should be consulted for minor complaints. If you need more professional attention and the issuing of prescription drugs, there are numerous private clinics in KL. An appointment is often available at short notice and a small fee will cover the cost of consultation. If prescription drugs are advised, the medicine is often available from the clinic itself.

KL is a fairly safe city but visitors should take commonsense precautions and not tempt pickpockets or snatch thieves by leaving wallets or purses exposed. In crowded places, especially the Petaling Street market and Puduraya bus station, keep your valuables in a secure place and be aware that pickpockets may be around. There have also been incidents of drink spiking. While people are generally friendly and it's a great place to let your hair down, it's best to stay alert, especially if you are out at night on your own.

Have a list of your traveller's cheque numbers and keep this with your proof of purchase and the contact number to use in case the cheques are lost or stolen. Keep this information separate from the cheques themselves; posting them to your email account is a good idea. Keep a photocopy of the main page of your passport and the page with the stamp of your Malaysian visa and keep these separate from your passport.

See page 139 for emergency contact telephone numbers.

OPENING HOURS

Large shops and department stores tend to open seven days a week at around 10.00 and close at 20.00. Government offices usually open 08.00–16.15 Monday to Friday, often closing for lunch 13.00–14.00, and 08.00–12.45 Saturday. Friday is different and the lunch hour is extended to 14.45 to allow time for a visit to a mosque for Friday prayers.

TOILETS

Public toilets of the flush type are to be found in all the shopping centres and in most cases are kept reasonably clean. Sometimes there are toilets of the squat type, especially in local restaurants and cafés. Toilet paper is usually provided, but you cannot always rely on it being available and so it is a good idea to carry a small supply of your own. Many travellers prefer to make use of hotels' flush toilets – all hotel lobbies will have such toilets.

CHILDREN

There are several places in KL which will keep the little ones occupied:

Aquaria Close encounters with sharks and other forms of marine life. The shark-feeding sessions are a highlight, but best avoid the Saturday shows due to the crowds. A colourful and exciting experience for children of most ages. Aquaria can be accessed via a path on the concourse level of Suria KLCC. ⓐ Concourse Level, Kuala Lumpur Convention Centre, Jalan Penang ⓣ (03) 2333 1888 ⓦ www.klaquaria.com ⓛ 11.00–20.00 (last admission 19.00).

🔺 *The dizzying Cosmo's World*

Daily feeding sessions: 12.00, 14.30 & 15.00. Shark-feeding sessions: 15.00 Mon, Wed & Sat. Admission charge

Cosmo's World An indoor theme park with over a dozen rides divided into the Galaxy Station for teenagers (and adults who want to be teenagers) and the Fantasy Garden for younger children. ⓐ Level 5, Berjaya Times Square, Jalan Imbi ⓣ (03) 2117 3118 ⓛ 12.00–22.00 Mon–Fri, 11.00–22.00 Sat & Sun ⓝ KL Monorail: Imbi

National Planetarium Children over the age of 12 should enjoy the large-format movies, planetarium and laser shows and the space-ball simulation. ⓐ 53 Jalan Perdana ⓣ (03) 2273 4303 ⓦ www.angkasa.gov.my ⓛ 09.30–16.30 Tues–Sun ⓝ KTM: Sentral. Admission charge

Toy City One of the largest toy shops in central Kuala Lumpur, packed with glossy playthings and gadgets. ⓐ 222B, Ramlee Mall, Suria KLCC ⓣ (03) 2166 3666 ⓛ 10.00–22.00 ⓝ Rapid KL Kelana Jaya Line: KLCC

Zoo Negara Children will like getting up close and personal with the animals at Malaysia's National Zoo (see page 122).

COMMUNICATIONS
Internet
Internet access is available throughout the city, either through internet shops or from your hotel. As with the making of phone calls from your hotel, the rates charged are usually exorbitant and it pays to go outside and use an internet shop. In the Bukit Bintang area, there is one on the third level of Sungei Wang and there is also one just around the corner on Jalan Sultan Ismail, on the second floor at No. 59, just past the 7-Eleven store and indicated by a shabby internet sign; the shop opens from

10.00–01.00. You can also make inexpensive international phone calls here. Chinatown is the next best area for finding shops offering internet access at reasonable rates.

Phone

Public telephones are easy to find – though it is equally easy to discover ones that are out of order – and for local calls you can use 10- or 20-sen coins if the phone accepts coins. It is more convenient, for local and international calls, to use a public phone that accepts a phonecard. Public phones are operated and owned by different service providers and therefore only accept that company's particular phonecard. The most common phonecard is Telekom Malaysia's iTalk card and to use it you will need to find an iTalk public phone. The iTalk card is available in denominations

TELEPHONING MALAYSIA

To telephone Malaysia from abroad, dial the international access code first (00), then the country code for Malaysia (60), then the area code for Kuala Lumpur, (03), followed by the local eight-digit number.

TELEPHONING ABROAD

To make an international call from Malaysia, dial 00, the international access code, then the country code, followed by the local area code minus the first 0, and then the number. Country codes: Australia 61; New Zealand 64; South Africa 27; USA & Canada 1; Republic of Ireland 353; UK 44.

⬥ *Ensure you have the correct phonecard*

of RM10, RM20, RM30 and RM50 and can be used to make international and domestic calls. Another option is to purchase a generic phonecard called an IDD card that can be used on any public phones and fixed lines for local and international calls. Both iTalk and IDD cards can be purchased in 7-Eleven outlets and from most kiosks selling newspapers. For domestic directory enquiries and for assistance with international calls call ① 101.

You should be able to make and receive calls and text messages using your mobile phone, but check with your home network before departure to make sure this is the case in Malaysia. Check, too, the cost of calls, because prices can be exorbitantly high.

Post

KL's **General Post Office** (ⓐ Dayabumi Complex, Jalan Sultan Hishamuddin ① (03) 8886 5000 ⓦ www.pos.com.my ① 08.30–18.00) is across the river from Central Market and not the most convenient place to reach on foot. Packages can be sent, though, from the post office on the second floor of Sungei Wang, and there is also a post office at basement level in Suria KLCC. Stamps to send postcards anywhere around the world cost 50 sen, letters less than 20 grams cost RM1.50, and stamps can usually be purchased from hotels. Overseas airmail takes between four and seven days to reach its destination; packages sent by surface mail will take up to two months.

ELECTRICITY

Mains voltage is the normal European one of 220V, 50 Hz, which means European appliances will work without a problem.

Equipment using 110V will require a converter. Plugs are usually of the three square-pin type, as in Britain. See ⓦ www.kropla.com for more information.

TRAVELLERS WITH DISABILITIES

Kuala Lumpur is not geared up for travellers with disabilities. Museums, mosques and other places of interest are not well equipped for wheelchair-using travellers and negotiating the consistently uneven pavements is a major problem. Toilets for the disabled are rare and public transport does not bear in mind the needs of travellers with disabilities. A guide to international airlines and airports and the facilities they offer for people with disabilities can be found at ⓦ www.allgohere.com.

All KL Hop-on Hop-off buses (see page 58) are wheelchair-friendly and are a convenient way to see the city. Suria KLCC (see page 98) is considered to be one of the most wheelchair-friendly shopping malls in the city.

TOURIST INFORMATION

Tourist Information Centre The national tourist office on Jalan Ampang covers the whole of Malaysia and is well worth visiting if you want to find out more about holiday destinations on the peninsula and in Sarawak and Sabah in East Malaysia.

Malaysia Tourism Centre ⓐ 109 Jalan Ampang ⓣ (03) 9235 4848 ⓛ 08.00–22.00 ⓝ KL Monorail: Bukit Nanas

A tourist information office is also located in the arrivals hall of KLIA (ⓛ 09.00–21.00) and on level 2 at KL Sentral (ⓣ (03) 2274 3125 ⓛ 09.00–18.00).

Websites
www.mtc.gov.my is the official website for the Malaysia
Tourism Centre.
www.tourismmalaysia.gov.my gives tourist information.
www.NST.com.my Online news from the English-language
The New Straits Times newspaper.
www.virtualmalaysia.com Tourist and travel information.

BACKGROUND READING
Forgotten Wars by Christoper Bayly and Tim Harper.
A comprehensive account of the historical background to
the emergence of modern Malaysia.
Culture Shock! Malaysia by Heidi Muran. An introduction
to the three races making up the country's population.
The Malay Dilemma by Mahathir Mohamad. Ex-prime minister
Mahathir Mohamad provides a remarkably honest account
of the politics behind Malaysia's Chinese-Malay mix.
Asian Cookbook by Charmaine Soloman. Try your hand at
recreating some Malay, Chinese or Indian dishes.
The Practical Encyclopedia of Asian Cooking by Sallie Morris and
deh-Ta Hsiung. More recipes that offer a flavour of Malaysia.

Emergencies

EMERGENCY NUMBERS
Police & Ambulance ⓣ 999
Fire ⓣ 994
Tourist Police ⓣ (03) 2149 6590

MEDICAL EMERGENCIES
General Hospital ⓐ Jalan Pahang ⓣ (03) 2692 1044
ⓘ Foreigners are only permitted in an emergency
Gleneagles Hospital ⓐ 282-6 Jalan Ampang ⓣ (03) 4257 1300
ⓦ gimc.com.my

   These two hospitals have 24-hour emergency services and
the Gleneagles Hospital also has a dental clinic. Doctors and
dentists at private clinics (see page 130) all speak English.

   The **Twin Towers Medical Centre** (ⓐ Level 4, Suria KLCC
ⓣ (03) 2382 3500 ⓦ www.ttmcklcc.com.my ⓒ 08.30–18.00
Mon–Sat) is able to dispense most of the medicines its doctors
prescribe and, if not immediately available, will obtain them
as quickly as possible.

POLICE
Hot line ⓣ (03) 2149 6590; enquiries: ⓣ (03) 2149 6593
Ampang station ⓣ (03) 4289 7222
Dang Wangi station ⓣ (03) 2691 2222

INDEX

SPOTTED YOUR NEXT CITY BREAK?

... then these CitySpots will have you in the know in no time, wherever you're heading.

Covering 100 cities worldwide, these vibrant pocket guides are packed with practical listings and imaginative suggestions, making sure you get the most out of your break, whatever your taste or budget.

Available from all good bookshops, your local Thomas Cook travel store or browse and buy online at www.thomascookpublishing.com

Thomas Cook Publishing

Editorial/project management: Lisa Plumridge
Copy editor: Paul Hines
Layout/DTP: Alison Rayner

The publishers would like to thank the following individuals and organisations for supplying their copyright photographs for this book: HNYQA/BgiStockPhoto.com, page 11; Pat Levy, pages 9, 15, 17, 23, 27, 39, 40, 42, 119 & 124; Pictures Colour Library, pages 45, 47 & 127; World Pictures/Photoshot, page 112; YTL Hotels & Properties Sdn. Bhd., page 34; Mark Bassett/The Source, all others.

Send your thoughts to
books@thomascook.com

- Found a great bar, club, shop or must-see sight that we don't feature?
- Like to tip us off about any information that needs a little updating?
- Want to tell us what you love about this handy little guidebook and more importantly how we can make it even handier?

Then here's your chance to tell all! Send us ideas, discoveries and recommendations today and then look out for your valuable input in the next edition of this title.

Email the above address (stating the title) or write to:
CitySpots Series Editor, Thomas Cook Publishing, PO Box 227, Coningsby Road, Peterborough PE3 8SB, UK.